Docu............   ....ory

Kevin Jefferys

Faculty of Arts and Education, University of Plymouth

The Labour Party

This fascinating book brings together a collection of original documents, many previously unpublished, which trace the history of the Labour Party from its electoral zenith in 1951, through the disasters and divisions of the early 1980s to the Party's apparent revival under Tony Blair. Focusing on how competing elements within the Party responded to persistent electoral failure, it indicates the extent to which the original vision of 'socialism' was consequently transformed. The documents show how the leadership and Party members in the constituencies profoundly disagreed over the political implications of post-war social change. They further demonstrate that Labour's 'socialism' has always been a contested concept, the meaning of which divided as much as united the Party faithful.

Steven Fielding is a Lecturer in the Department of Politics and Contemporary History, University of Salford

Documents in Contemporary History is a series designed for sixth-formers and undergraduates in higher education: it aims to provide both an overview of specialist research on topics in post-1939 British history and a wide-ranging selection of primary source material.

Already published

Alan Booth *British economic development since 1945*

Stephen Brooke *Reform and reconstruction: Britain after the war, 1945–51*

Kevin Jefferys *War and reform: British politics during the Second World War*

Ritchie Ovendale *British defence policy since 1945*

Scott Lucas *Britain and Suez: the lion's last roar*

Harold L. Smith *Britain in the Second World War: a social history*

Sean Greenwood *Britain and European integration since the Second World War*

John Baylis *Anglo-American relations: the rise and fall of the special relationship*

Forthcoming

Rodney Lowe *The classic welfare state in Britain*
Stuart Ball *The Conservative Party, 1940–1992*
Ralph Negrine *The British media since 1945*

Documents in Contemporary History

The Labour Party
'Socialism' and society
since 1951

Edited by
Steven Fielding

Lecturer, Department of Politics and Contemporary History, University of Salford

Manchester University Press
Manchester and New York
Distributed exclusively in the USA by St. Martin's Press

Copyright © Steven Fielding 1997

Published by Manchester University Press
Oxford Road, Manchester M13 9NR, UK
and Room 400, 175 Fifth Avenue, New York, NY 10010, USA

Distributed exclusively in the USA
by St. Martin's Press, Inc., 175 Fifth Avenue, New York,
NY 10010, USA

British Library Cataloguing-in-Publication Data
A catalogue record for this book is available from the British Library

Library of Congress Cataloging-in-Publication Data
The Labour Party. 'Socialism' and society since 1951 / edited by Steven
  Fielding.
      p.   cm. – (Documents in contemporary history)
    Includes bibliographical references.
    ISBN 0-7190-4269-0. – ISBN 0-7190-4270-4
    1. Labour Party (Great Britain)   2. Great Britain–Politics and
  government–1945-   I. Fielding, Steven (Steven J.). 1961–
  II. Series.
  JN1129.L32L27   1997   96-32159
  324.24107'09'045–dc20   CIP

First published 1997

00 99 98 97   10 9 8 7 6 5 4 3 2 1

Printed by Bell & Bain Ltd, Glasgow

Contents

Acknowledgements

As Neil Kinnock might have put it, thanks for aid, advice and accommodation are due to: Lindsay Abbot and Nigel Parker, Stephen Bird, Andy Flinn, Kevin Jefferys, Nick Tiratsoo, Jon Tonge, those librarians and archivists responsible for the welfare of local Labour Party records and the individual Labour members who spent the time and energy producing all the sources included in this volume.

The author would like to thank the University of Salford Christopher Hale Fund for covering certain travel expenses.

Acknowledgement is also due to the following for their kind permission to quote the relevant selections: the Labour Party Archive, National Museum of Labour History, Manchester (1.1–3, 1.11, 1.12, 2.3–5, 2.11, 2.12, 3.3, 3.8 3.16, 4.1, 4.4, 4.8, 5.8, 5.12, 6.2, 6.5, 6.11); Quartet Books (1.7); the estate of Hugh Dalton and Jonathan Cape (1.9); the estate of Anthony Crosland and Jonathan Cape (1.12); Lord Jenkins of Putney (1.14, 4.5); Lord Jenkins of Putney and Lucie Hauser (5.4); Lord Rodgers of Quarry Bank (1.15, 2.8, 5.10); Mrs Margaret Simey and Merseyside Record Office (1.17); the Historians' Press and Lady Gordon Walker (2.6); Tameside Local Studies Library (2.10, 3.14); West Yorkshire Archive Service, Calderdale (2.9, 4.2); Joyce Roberts (3.19); Stuart Holland and Quartet Books (4.3); *Political Quarterly* (4.9); Warrington Trades Union Council (4.10); Heretic Books and Peter Tatchell, who retains world copyright, 1983 (5.5); Michael Foot and HarperCollins Publishers Limited (5.11); Greene and Heaton Limited, copyright Bryan Gould, 1995 (6.13); Verso Books (6.14); *Tribune* (7.8); Tony Blair MP and the Fabian Society (7.3).

All efforts have been made to contact owners of other copyright material.

Chronology of major events

1951
October   General election: Conservatives   321 seats
                              Labour   295 seats
                              Liberals   6 seats
                              Conservative majority: 17

1952
October   Labour conference exposes rift between leadership and Bevanite constituency parties

1954
April   Aneurin Bevan resigns from shadow cabinet

1955
March   Bevan narrowly avoids expulsion from the Parliamentary Labour Party
May   General election: Conservatives   345 seats
                              Labour   277 seats
                              Liberals   6 seats
                              Conservative majority: 54
December   Hugh Gaitskell elected leader

1956
February   Bevan becomes shadow foreign secretary to mark reconciliation with Gaitskell
May   Victory for Socialism revived

1959
October   General election: Conservatives   317 seats
                              Labour   258 seats
                              Liberals   9 seats
                              Conservative majority: 100
November   Gaitskell calls for the revision of clause iv

1960

March   Gaitskell permitted by National Executive Committee to add a further statement to clause iv but not to change the clause itself

July   Bevan dies

October   Labour conference supports unilateralism; Harold Wilson fails in his challenge to Gaitskell

November   Campaign for Democratic Socialism formed

1961

October   Labour conference reverses decision on unilateralism

1963

January   Gaitskell dies

February   Wilson elected leader

September   Wilson delivers 'white heat' speech to Labour conference

1964

October   General election:

Labour	317	seats
Conservatives	304	seats
Liberals	9	seats
Labour majority:	5	

1965

July   'July measures' deflate economy and cut government spending to defend sterling

1966

March   General election:

Labour	363	seats
Conservatives	253	seats
Liberals	12	seats
Labour majority:	96	

July   'July measures' are further deflationary measures to prevent devaluation of sterling

1967

November   Government forced to devalue sterling, causing a political crisis for Labour

1968

February   Commonwealth Immigration Act passed to restrict immigration of persecuted Kenyan Asians, despite opposition within the Party

1969
January   'In Place of Strife' made public to dismay within Party
June   Wilson and Barbara Castle forced by union and Party pressure to back down over 'In Place of Strife'

1970
June

General election:		
Conservatives	330 seats
Labour	287 seats
Liberals	6 seats
Conservative majority:	30

John Smith and Neil Kinnock elected MPs for first time

1973
October   Campaign for Labour Party Democracy formed

1974
February

General election:		
Labour	301 seats
Conservatives	297 seats
Liberals	14 seats
Labour majority:	-34

October

General election:		
Labour	319 seats
Conservatives	277 seats
Liberals	13 seats
Labour majority:	3

1976
April   James Callaghan elected leader
October   Callaghan tells Party conference that inflation, not unemployment, is the main economic enemy; government forced to borrow $3.9 billion from the International Monetary Fund to stave off economic crisis

1979
January   'Winter of discontent' strike wave
April

General election:		
Conservatives	339 seats
Labour	269 seats
Liberals	11 seats
Conservative majority:	43

1980
October   Labour conference votes for unilateralism, mandatory re-selection of MPs and to take away the exclusive right of the Parliamentary Labour Party to elect leader
November   Michael Foot elected leader, the last by MPs only

1981

January   Special conference gives unions a 40 per cent say in election of Labour leader

March   Social Democratic Party formed by four Labour ex-ministers

September   Tony Benn fails to depose Denis Healey as deputy leader

1983

June

General election: Conservatives	397 seats
Labour	209 seats
SDP/Liberal alliance	23 seats
Conservative majority:	144

Tony Blair elected MP for first time

October   Neil Kinnock elected leader

1984

March   Miners' strike begins

1985

March   Miners' strike ends in defeat for the National Union of Mineworkers

October   Kinnock makes his 'Militant' speech at conference

1987

June

General election: Conservatives	376 seats
Labour	229 seats
SDP/Liberal alliance	22 seats
Conservative majority:	102

October   Policy Review initiated

1988

October   Tony Benn fails to depose Kinnock as leader

1989

October   Policy Review finalised and passed by Labour conference

1992

April

General election: Conservatives	336 seats
Labour	271 seats
Liberal Democrats	20 seats
Conservative majority:	21

October   John Smith elected leader

1993
October   Conference supports one member one vote in selection of parliamentary candidates

1994
May   John Smith dies
June   Tony Blair elected leader
October   Blair calls for the revision of clause iv

1995
April   Special conference votes to abolish old clause iv
November   MORI opinion poll places support for Labour at 56 per cent, with the Conservatives at 26 per cent

Introduction

In the early 1950s the Labour Party hoped to transform British society through the implementation of 'socialist' policies; instead, by the 1990s, society had forced Labour to change its programme to such an extent that many no longer considered it at all 'socialist'. As with all generalisations, this statement requires justification, elaboration and some qualification. Even so, it conveniently summarises Labour's history since 1951 and is the basis for this collection of documents.

Labour left office in October 1951 committed to maintain and, when possible, extend the achievements of the Attlee governments of 1945–51. Establishing what would later be described as state collectivism, Labour in power had built a welfare state and nationalised one-fifth of the economy. Such policies appeared to work: the incoming Conservatives inherited an expanding economy with full employment and a society in which poverty seemed to be on the wane.[1] Thus, confidence in the beneficent effect of both state intervention in the economy and the collectivist approach to social policy underpinned Labour thinking, despite the loss of power. After all, such policies were, it seemed, popular: in 1951 Labour won 48.8 per cent of all votes cast, a higher proportion than even the victorious Conservatives. Therefore, most members of the Labour Movement entered the 1950s with a clear vision of the future and a firm belief in their Party's ability to realise it.

Such certainty was undermined during the 1950s as Labour found it increasingly difficult to win back power and so apply its policies and build 'socialism'. A handful of victories in the 1960s and 1970s notwithstanding, this problem refused to go away. Labour's electoral shortcomings cannot be stressed enough: between 1951 and 1992 the Party won only four out of twelve general elections (see Table 1). Only one of these victories – that achieved in 1966 – gave the Party a secure Commons majority. In total, between 1951 and 1996, Labour held office for only eleven years.

Naturally enough, Party members have tried to understand the reasons for this appalling performance. Over the years, there have been two basic responses. Some complained that faithfully adhering to policies which seemed to lose votes made little sense. Labour, they suggested, needed to 'revise' (in the 1950s) or 'modernise' (in the 1980s) its programme in order to become more acceptable to the electorate. Others disagreed. They believed there to be little point in Labour standing for office if it had abandoned what they took to be 'socialism'. Their assumption was that unreconstructed state collectivism remained a potential vote winner. They believed the real problem was that the Party's parliamentary leaders had lost faith; they needed to regain their radical zeal or be replaced.

This differentiated response to electoral failure was based on contrasting interpretations of post-war social change and its political consequences. Broadly speaking, some – Labour's parliamentary leadership in particular – accepted one view; others – especially many active members in the constituencies – adhered to another. By the late 1950s Labour's leaders believed that as society was increasingly affluent and individualistic, so support for state collectivism was diminishing. If it was to remain electable, Labour, they stated, needed to take account of these developments by changing its policies. Supporters of the rival analysis considered that continuity was more advantageous than change. Britain, they believed, remained a divided society in which class privilege prevented the majority reaching their full potential. Therefore, they suggested, Labour's traditional 'socialist' vision and the state collectivist programme through which it was to be achieved remained vitally relevant.

Over the years, increasingly after 1987 especially, the former view prevailed decisively over the latter. By the late 1980s Labour had distanced itself from many of the policies that had been widely accepted in the early 1950s. Yet, as the 1992 general

Table 1. Labour's electoral performance, 1951–92

	Total vote	*% share of votes cast*	*Difference from previous election*
1951	13,948,605	48.8	–
1955	12,404,970	46.4	-2.4
1959	12,215,538	43.8	-2.6
1964	12,205,814	44.1	+0.3
1966	13,064,951	47.9	+3.8
1970	12,179,341	43.0	-4.9
1974	11,639,243	37.1	-5.9
1974	11,457,079	39.2	+2.1
1979	11,532,148	36.9	-2.3
1983	8,456,934	27.6	-9.3
1987	10,029,944	30.8	+3.2
1992	11,559,735	34.4	+3.6

Source: D. Butler and D. Kavanagh, *The British General Election of 1992*, London, 1992.

election demonstrated, even this was insufficient to win power. As Tony Blair declared on numerous occasions after becoming leader in 1994: continued social change meant that the Party had to transform itself further, into what he called New Labour. This did not mean, he reassured members, that they needed to abandon those moral values which had underpinned state collectivism. Instead, remaining true to such ethics, Labour needed to pursue policies more appropriate to the contemporary scene. In a similar vein, Blair's deputy, John Prescott, talked of the need to place 'traditional values in a modern setting'. Others were less sanguine. They complained that Blair, like his immediate predecessors John Smith and Neil Kinnock, had abandoned all hope of achieving 'socialism' in order to enter government.

Thus, to qualify, slightly, the opening sentence of this Introduction, it was a particular *perception* of post-war social change, one especially favoured by Labour's parliamentary leaders, that had transformed the Party by the 1990s.

II

The documents gathered here concentrate on three related themes, each of which furthers our understanding of how and why the Labour Party responded in the way it did to its electoral difficulties. This volume does not, therefore, cover each and every aspect of Labour's recent history. Certain topics have been ignored because they detract from the focus adopted here. In particular, foreign affairs have been all but excluded. Whilst the Cold War, decolonisation, the Vietnam War, apartheid, the European Community and unilateral nuclear disarmament often divided the Party's ranks, they rarely directly influenced Labour's performance at the polls. Few voters, in contrast to most Labour members, considered such issues important.

Having indicated what this collection does not contain, it is now appropriate to outline the three themes highlighted in the documents. First, Party members have been constantly at odds over which social groups the Party needed to attract most if it was to win power. As already indicated, some saw the post-war period as one of rapid social change. In particular, the unskilled manual – often referred to as the 'traditional' – working class declined in number as they were replaced by skilled and semi-skilled 'affluent' workers. There was also an increase in white-collar or 'intermediate' occupations. This view was substantiated by the researches of many sociologists and political scientists. They considered that these trends reduced the number of Labour's 'natural' supporters and increased that part of the electorate more inclined to Conservative policies.[2]

This kind of social change should not necessarily have caused Labour too many problems. The Party constitution stated that Labour represented 'workers by hand or brain': in the 1940s the leadership described Labour as the 'people's Party', concerned to advance the interests of the vast majority of the nation.[3] Such an appeal was never far from the lips of Labour's later leaders: they were conscious of the need to maximise support across the classes. Harold Wilson was perhaps the most successful in this respect. His 'white heat' rhetoric in 1963–64 generated support amongst lower-middle-class voters, although neither the rhetoric nor the appeal lasted long.[4] There were many in the Party uncomfortable with Wilson's attempt to woo middle-class voters.

Disputing the suggestion that the working class had, in any real sense, been transformed, they also thought that Labour's first – and in some cases only – duty lay in furthering the interests of the trade union movement. Labour needed to stay close to its roots: the Party's close historical and organisational links with many unions gave force to this point of view.[5]

In the early 1980s some members called for Labour to identify more closely with oppressed minorities – such as gays, the inner-city poor and ethnic groups – and leave to the Conservatives the task of garnering the votes of skilled workers and the middle class. In contrast, after 1983 the Kinnock leadership stressed, again and again, the need to win the support of more than a combination of the 'traditional' working class and disparate minorities. Tony Blair's appeal to 'middle England' and his shadow chancellor Gordon Brown's reference to the 'decent hard-working majority' are merely the latest expressions of this emphasis.

Such distinct electoral priorities were inextricably linked to the second theme running through this collection: disagreements over domestic policy. In practice, these disputes mostly revolved around competing views of the role of the state in the economy and society. As the period developed, Attlee's state collectivism was increasingly criticised by Party leaders, who noted its apparent electoral unpopularity. In moving the Party away from such an approach, however, they faced something of a problem. Clause iv, section 4 of Labour's constitution committed the Party:

> To secure for the workers by hand or brain the full fruits of their industry and the most equitable distribution thereof that may be possible upon the basis of the common ownership of the means of production, distribution and exchange, and the best obtainable system of popular administration and control of each industry or service.

The most popular interpretation of this clause, first drafted in 1918, was that in principle Labour was bound to extend state control of the economy whenever possible.[6] After three successive election defeats Hugh Gaitskell took the bull by the horns in 1959 and sought to change the clause so it could no longer be read in such a way. By so doing he hoped to reverse Labour's declining appeal. Despite causing much disruption, Gaitskell failed and for the next thirty years or so the Party remained notionally committed to pushing the frontiers of the state ever forward. In practice, however, Gaitskell's successors ignored the clause and in 1995 Tony Blair reworded it so he could show voters that Labour had truly become New Labour.

The Labour governments of the 1960s and 1970s found that Britain's economic weaknesses hampered one of their chief ambitions, the reduction of inequality – that, for some, *was* 'socialism'. Increased state spending on welfare – thought to be the main way to overcome social injustice – was financed through taxation. In the 1950s Labour leaders hoped that a booming economy would finance such expenditure by expanding revenues, obviating the need to increase tax rates. Despite their hopes, Britain's economy, which under-performed even at the best of times, was hit by a world recession in the 1970s. The 1974–79 Labour government was consequently forced to reduce its social welfare programme as well as increase tax rates simply to maintain basic services. This problem was exacerbated when public sector unions won wage rises, as such gains could be financed only by taxpayers. When Labour ministers tried to resist such claims, they only provoked strikes along with the disaffection of union leaders and Party members, culminating in the 1978–79 'winter of discontent'.

Despite the protestations of James Callaghan, Labour's beleaguered Prime Minister between 1976 and 1979, many Party members discounted his problems. These critics stated that if only Labour implemented clause iv, voters would eventually support nationalisation. Those hostile to the leadership also suggested that ministers short of revenue could either finance welfare by cutting spending on areas such as defence or raise taxes on the rich and middle class. Wage increases for public employees were also considered well deserved, as most were badly paid: the better off could afford to pay more tax for this too.

The third theme highlighted in this collection is Labour's problematic organisation. Practically, if Labour was to win power, it needed enough willing and eager members to put the Party's case across to the people and ensure supporters voted at elections. Party members were, however, responsible for more than electoral work: they also chose parliamentary candidates and contributed to policy discussions by submitting resolutions and sending delegates to Labour's annual conference. Members holding posts in local parties and those who participated most keenly in election work as well as policy debates were known – often derogatively – as activists. This body was usually critical of Labour's parliamentary leaders, who were thought too moderate and keen to place pragmatism before principle. Activists were also frustrated by their limited voice within the organisation. They argued that they were responsible for putting Labour MPs into the Commons but had little subsequent influence over them or any resulting Labour government. The general management committee (GMC) of each constituency Labour party (CLP), by definition composed only of active members, was formally empowered to select its own prospective parliamentary candidate (PPC) or deselect a sitting MP. However, it proved enormously difficult for a GMC to be rid of an MP even if they came fundamentally to disagree with one another. During the early 1980s changes which made deselection much easier were passed at conference: this gave more power to activists. To reverse this, in the later 1980s Neil Kinnock introduced the first of a number of counter-reforms. These were described as democratic by the leadership, but others thought their real purpose was to weaken the power of activists by giving a bigger say to ordinary Party members. This latter group, it was widely believed, generally supported the leadership's viewpoint. Thus, under severe pressure from John Smith, in 1993 conference decided that when it came to selection or deselection, all members of a CLP had to be balloted, not just those who ran the GMC.

III

Before proceeding further, it might help those unfamiliar with the Labour Party to indicate something of its most salient characteristics during the period under review.

One cliché, still favoured in the middle 1990s, has it that Labour was and remains a 'broad church'. This is meant to suggest that – despite their different social origins, position in the Party organisation and strength of support for particular policies and specific tactics – all Labour members find agreement on fundamentals. Members are all, to varying degrees perhaps, 'socialists'. This begs the vital question: what does a 'socialist' believe in? This is by no means clear, hence the quotation marks around the word throughout this volume. Unfortunately, whilst definitions of the term are easy to come by, they are even easier to disagree about. As good a one as any is: socialists believe that society must be reformed because of its domination by what they take to be an unfair and inefficient economic system – capitalism – in order to achieve a greater degree of social justice which, left to its own devices, capitalism would never produce. It would be surprising if any Labour member past or present would argue with this form of words. Yet, whilst characterising Party members' general outlook, even this definition takes us only so far. In the past, as much as today, there have been differences over the means, extent and object of reform. With regard to means, there have always been some who thought that increased public ownership of the economy was the prerequisite to social justice; some suggested that it could be best achieved through spending on welfare services; others indicated that improved access to high-quality education was the key; another group thought that leaving trade unions free to increase workers' wages was the best means. More recently, Tony Blair and his supporters have suggested that social justice cannot be achieved through state action alone: individuals have to be encouraged to take more responsibility for their own lives. Within these contrasting approaches have been located disagreements over how much reform can be introduced at any one time and, indeed, what level is ultimately desirable. Some members have thought it necessary to modify capitalism relatively little to achieve their ends; others have sought to replace it totally. There have also been different opinions over what type of inequality needs to be tackled most keenly: for a long time the object of reform was seen to be the working class; latterly there have been advocates of the need to deal with inequalities originating from differences of gender, sexuality and ethnicity. The extent to which definitions of 'socialism' have varied between individuals and over time cannot be stressed enough.

If Labour since 1951 can be described as a 'broad church' it has been one in the same sense as contemporary Anglicanism.

Contained within Church of England ranks, it should be recalled, are liberal bishops who think the Bible contains metaphorical stories rather than a record of real historical events; side by side with them is a laity which includes fundamentalists who believe that each word is gospel. This is, after all, the Party described by cabinet minister Barbara Castle in 1968 as this 'curious movement with its curious contradictions'.[7] It is, then, inadequate to describe Labour as a 'broad church' and leave it at that. We must be more specific.

It could be said that there have always been, in effect, two Labour parties. One has been organised at Westminster and formed the opposition or government of the day; the other has been based in the country at large. The Parliamentary Labour Party (PLP) is constituted by all MPs elected under the Party's colours at general and by-elections. In opposition these MPs annually elect a shadow cabinet from which any initial Labour cabinet is formed. Until 1981 MPs also enjoyed an exclusive say in the election of the Party leader. Even now, a leadership candidate must be an MP and needs to be nominated by at least 12.5 per cent of parliamentary colleagues. In 1983 Neil Kinnock was the first leader to be elected by an electoral college comprised of trade unions and other affiliated bodies (40 per cent), MPs and MEPs (30 per cent) and CLPs (30 per cent). By the time of Tony Blair's election as leader in 1994 the proportions of each of the college's three components had been equalised so they all contributed one-third to the total vote.

Important though the PLP has been throughout this period, it has never constituted the Labour Party in its entirety. Labour's national organisation must also be taken into account. Since the late 1970s this has been found on Walworth Road in south London. Under the supervision of the National Executive Committee (NEC) the Party's national officers – such as its general secretary and directors of research, policy and communications – have been responsible for devising policy proposals, implementing decisions ratified by Labour's annual conference, maintaining the Party's constitution and conducting election campaigns. The role of Labour's nine regional offices has been to keep in close contact with local parties and, in concert with the national organisation, to which they are answerable, ensure that the Party is run as efficiently as possible.

The Party leader, deputy leader and general secretary automatically qualify as members of the NEC. Of the rest, twelve are directly elected by affiliated trade unions, seven by CLPs and one by affiliated socialist societies. A further six are elected by conference delegates. Because the unions have always contributed a majority of such delegates, they have controlled eighteen out of the twenty-nine NEC seats. Labour's conference is in theory the Party's sovereign body: only it can decide those policies that the NEC is expected to implement; only it can change the Party's constitution. It is necessary to emphasise that this is conference's formal role. In practice conference is often subordinate to the Party leadership, which can so construct a debate that a favourable result becomes almost certain. Moreover, increasingly since the later 1980s conference has, a few exceptions apart, obediently ratified most of the leader's wishes.[8]

Conference delegates are drawn from CLPs and organisations affiliated to the Party, which include the Fabian Society, Christian Socialist Movement, Labour Students, the Society of Labour Lawyers and the Co-Operative Society. The most important group of affiliated organisations has always been trade unions. For most of our period, trade unions controlled as much as 90 per cent of conference votes. Union dominance here was the result of the affiliation, at a discounted rate, of their members to Labour. This has been an important source of revenue for the Party. Given that most CLPs had members counted in their hundreds whilst many unions had them in hundreds of thousands, the numerical advantage always lay with the latter. Each union had its own procedures for deciding which way its votes should be cast. A number gave this responsibility to their annual or bi-annual conference, others to their executive committees, some to the delegation they sent to the conference. The result was often ambiguity and occasionally outright malpractice, to such an extent that it at least gave the appearance of being undemocratic. Once decided, each union would then cast all its members' votes in one block. Thus, to take one example, despite the fact that a union conference might have decided by merely one vote to support a particular policy, all the union's thousands of votes would be cast in one direction – hence the term 'block vote'. If an individual union cast its vote in a block then all unions did not act *en bloc*: unions differed over policy as much as ordinary Party members. The overweening role of the unions in the Party, but especially at conference, was a constant point of criticism. By the later 1980s the leadership, wishing to demonstrate to voters that Labour was not in the pocket of union bosses, campaigned to reduce the preponderance of the unions at conference. Initially many union leaders opposed this, warning that 'no say' would lead to 'no pay'. In the end, however, they were convinced that it was politically expedient to agree. In 1990 the union contribution to conference was reduced to 70 per cent of votes; in 1995 it was taken down further to 50 per cent. This finally gave the CLPs an equal standing with the unions.[9]

The elemental unit within Labour's organisation has always been the ward party, to which all individual members belong. It is in the ward that most have regular contact with the Party, should they decide to attend its monthly meetings. Each ward elects officers such as treasurer, chair and secretary, who try to maintain contact with members, increase their number, raise funds as well as fight local and national elections. Each ward also elects delegates to their CLP's GMC. This body controls the affairs of the CLP and tries to direct and coordinate activity within the constituency and between wards. As has been argued, it is at the ward and CLP level that the Party's electoral fate can ultimately be decided.[10] National policies may be good or bad, popular or unpopular, but if Labour supporters are not induced to vote – an important function of local parties – then the Party will never be able to implement them.

Whilst a CLP with a large membership does not necessarily mean that it is an efficient electoral organisation, it is broadly indicative of this. Moreover, the level of membership also says something about Labour's wider appeal, although this point should not be pushed too far: rising membership in a ward may simply be due to a group of dedicated individuals knocking on doors. Even so, members are an important resource – in financial and propaganda terms. Thus, Labour's declining membership since the early 1950s was of no small concern to the Party hierarchy. In 1952 individual membership stood at just over one million; by the early 1980s it hovered around the 250,000 mark. Since the election of Tony Blair as leader, membership has staged a modest recovery: at the end of 1995 it stood at 350,000.

Not only did membership decline over the period, but some also suggest that its social composition underwent profound change. It is hard to be precise about this: whilst there have been numerous surveys of particular wards and constituencies, there has been only one national survey. This matter is also complicated by the fact that membership figures are notoriously unreliable. Broadly speaking, however, women have consistently formed a minority: across the decades, about 40 per cent of members have been female. Such members have been eligible to form women's sections which affiliate to ward and constituency parties and so ensure them a distinct voice: until recently Labour women also held their own national conference. However, many sections were relatively unpolitical whilst not all female members wished to be part of what most male members saw as marginal bodies. Few women have been active members, although the proportion is probably higher now than it used to be. However, so low was the proportion of female Labour MPs that in the early 1990s the Party briefly supported women-only short lists in certain constituencies. This measure aroused much hostility and was subsequently dropped. In the past, Labour membership broadly reflected the fact that society had a manual-working-class majority; since the later 1960s, however, the Party has become progressively more middle class. Yet, even before this change, middle-class members held a disproportionate number of local and, especially, national Party posts. This domination has subsequently increased.

As mentioned earlier, activists are generally more to the left of their leaders and the wider membership. A very generous estimate would be that one-third of members can be defined as active. In the early 1970s, it has been suggested, this body became much more left wing than hitherto, owing to an influx of Marxist-influenced university-educated radicals.[11] Some of these were entryists, that is, they actually belonged to another political organisation whose strategy was to take over the Labour Party and use it for their own ends. Such organisations, usually influenced by the ideas of Leon Trotsky, were both small and unpopular: Militant Tendency was the most famous such group. Because of falling membership and the fact that entryists were geographically concentrated, they took over certain inner-city parties – most notoriously in Liverpool. As entryists denied they belonged to another organisation it was difficult to prove a person was not a genuine Labour member. Neil Kinnock took up the challenge and expelled a number of Militant leaders in the mid-1980s. Kinnock also hoped to increase membership in order to dilute the influence of such well organised vocal minorities and make Labour more representative of the population as a whole. Even so, as the only national survey of membership so far discovered, Labour members in the early 1990s were more likely to be: white (96 per cent), male (61 per cent), white-collar and professional workers (65 per cent), employed in the public sector (63 per cent) and over forty-five years of age (52 per cent).[12]

IV

This collection is divided into seven chapters, which proceed chronologically from the early 1950s to the mid-1990s.

As chapter one indicates, Labour appeared to be in good shape, despite losing the 1951 general election, which ended a period in which it had held power for six years. Whilst some were less sanguine, most members were confident that Labour would eventually establish 'socialism' (documents 1.1–4). Members were, nevertheless divided as to the best means of proceeding towards this end. There were, most significantly, differences over electoral strategy (1.5, 1.6) and ideology. Aneurin Bevan, who had resigned from the Labour cabinet in April 1951, appealed to many activists by stating that Labour's basic principles, the most prominent being the commitment to extend public ownership, were the key to electoral revival (1.7). Bevan's ideas won applause in the constituencies but aroused only the hostility of his parliamentary colleagues, especially that of the future leader Hugh Gaitskell (1.8). Divergent interpretations of social and economic change under Churchill's Conservative government of 1951–55 reflected these basic differences (1.9, 1.10). Whilst some attributed Labour's defeat in the 1955 general election to popular affluence, others looked to the poor state of Party organisation as the most significant factor (1.11). Despite this concern, little was done to improve matters. In any case, soon after this election Gaitskell succeeded Attlee and began to shift policy away from nationalisation. As the new leader's supporters indicated, this was due to the belief that, in the light of social and economic change, extending public ownership was no longer necessary. If 'socialism' could be defined as the reduction and eventual eradication of inequality, nationalisation was not the best means of doing so. In a context in which the economy was booming, differences between rich and poor could be ameliorated through government spending (1.12). Whilst disputes over the relative merits of nationalisation continued, others defined their 'socialism' in purely ethical, even religious, terms (1.13), an emphasis to be revisited by Tony Blair in the 1990s. The leadership's caution over public ownership galvanised members who remained firmly attached to state control. Those speaking for activists even blamed the pursuit of moderation for the Party's 1955 defeat. They called for more internal democracy, in particular the reduction of the unions' role at conference. Gaitskell supporters rejected such calls, not surprisingly given that they enjoyed the support of the biggest unions (1.14, 1.15). Thus, as the decade drew to a close, Labour looked two ways on policy whilst its organisation remained generally – if cosily – inefficient and, in some places, virtually moribund (1.16, 1.17).

As chapter two indicates, Gaitskell and his followers blamed Labour's third successive defeat, in 1959, on the Party's 'old-fashioned' image. They sought to make Labour appear more relevant to society (2.1). Others considered such analysis superficial: society needed to change, they said, not the Party (2.2). Notwithstanding this view, Gaitskell outlined his position at the 1959 conference. There he called for a substantial revision of Labour's commitment to extend public ownership, embodied in clause iv (2.3). This was rejected: too many members took it to symbolise their vision of 'socialism' (2.4). As a concession, Gaitskell was allowed to add a supplementary list of aims and values to the constitution (2.5). He considered this an insufficient response to social change and remained convinced of the need to transform the Party fundamentally. Gaitskell saw an opportunity to achieve this by crushing his activist critics over their support for unilateral nuclear disarmament (2.6, 2.7). Initially defeated on this, Gaitskell's supporters formed the Campaign for Democratic Socialism, which aimed to defeat unilateralism in the short term and eventually 'moderate' all Party policy (2.8). They were only partially successful: Gaitskell reversed support for unilateralism at Labour's 1961 conference, but failed to change Labour's fundamental character. During this moment of intense conflict, the Party also attempted to improve its appeal to voters, especially housewives, thought to have voted Conservative in 1959 because of their liking for consumerism (2.9). In fact, the Party changed little during this period. Despite various initiatives, Labour continued to be run by an active minority, some of whom were reluctant to see it include those other than manual workers (2.10–12). Nevertheless, Gaitskell's death in 1963 was seen by some partisans to have been a decisive turning point in the history of the Labour Party (2.13).

Chapter three deals with Labour's most electorally successful period since 1951. Gaitskell's sudden death led to the election of Harold Wilson. Wilson aroused loathing amongst the former leader's supporters owing to his perceived character failings and Bevanite past (3.1). Even so, Wilson broadly accepted Gaitskell's analysis of the political consequences of social change and tried to make the Party appear more relevant to affluent voters (3.2). Others remained convinced that Labour's prime purpose was to serve the interests of the trade union movement (3.3). Despite these abiding differences, in 1964 Labour entered office having promised to establish a 'New Britain' (3.4). The Labour government's small Commons majority and the country's economic problems meant Wilson achieved little, simply surviving in office (3.5, 3.6). In March 1966, however, he won re-election with a large majority. This generated an expectation that Labour would fulfil Wilson's earlier promise (3.7, 3.8). Further economic difficulties soon brought optimists back to earth (3.9). In response to this crisis, the government cut spending on social programmes and tried to limit wage increases. These priorities demoralised many Party members and Labour's organisation suffered as a consequence (3.10, 3.11). The government's attempt to limit the immigration of Kenyan Asians also aroused bad feeling in the ranks (3.12, 3.13). Trade unionists were especially critical of the government's economic policies, which they considered interfered with their own affairs (3.14). This alienation was exacerbated by the introduction of 'In Place of Strife', Barbara Castle's response to a wave of unofficial strikes in vital industries (3.15). Her proposals aroused so much opposition within cabinet, PLP and unions that Castle backed down, much to the relief of many members (3.16). The issue exposed one more of Labour's divisions: was it a Party of the 'national' or the trade union interest (3.17)? Given all of the above problems, it is not surprising that Wilson lost the 1970 general election. He blamed this defeat as well as his government's modest achievements on external factors, in particular Britain's persistent economic weakness (3.18). In contrast, critics on the left blamed Wilson's failure on his complete lack of adherence to 'socialist' policies (3.19).

As chapter four reveals, after 1970 Wilson paid dearly for turning his back on the trade unions whilst in government. The 1970 conference, reflecting the views of most activists, forced the leadership to support unions in their struggles with the Conservative government (4.1, 4.2). In concert with this shift came an increased demand for a greater emphasis on nationalisation within Labour's programme (4.3). Wilson was unable to resist such pressure, as was evident in Labour's manifesto of February 1974 (4.4). From this election Labour emerged as the largest Party in the Commons but one bereft of a majority. A second election in October gave Wilson a majority of only three seats. This government faced economic problems more severe than the ones confronted in the 1960s: a world slump caused unemployment to rise whilst continued union demands saw inflation increase alarmingly. Ironically, such difficulties were welcomed by Labour's Trotskyist entryists, seeing in them the final collapse of capitalism (4.5). The basis of the 1974–79 government's strategy was the 'social contract', in which ministers pledged to improve spending on social programmes of benefit to working-class families in return for some sort of wage restraint on the part of the trade unions. Right from the start difficulties were evident. Ministers emphasised only the latter aspect of the contract whilst union leaders highlighted the former (4.6, 4.7). This problem of interpretation multiplied under Wilson's successor, James Callaghan. Forced to borrow huge sums from the International Monetary Fund, Callaghan was obliged both to reduce social expenditure and to resist wage demands (4.8). In the midst of this crisis a number of Gaitskell's former supporters began to blame the country's dire economic performance on the power of government itself. From being a solution, the state was now seen to be the problem (4.9). On the other hand, union activists were increasingly hostile to the government's attempts to hold down wages: according to them the workers were being forced to sacrifice their standard of living to maintain capitalism (4.10). Despite such problems, some of Callaghan's embattled ministers considered that, in the circumstances, they had introduced some useful reforms (4.11). Unfortunately, the 1978–79 'winter of discontent' demonstrated Callaghan's inability to control wage-driven inflation (4.12). He was ultimately forced to call a general election through losing a no-confidence vote forced by disaffected Scottish Nationalists (4.13). Labour lost the subsequent election, held in April 1979. Callaghan had done his best to 'moderate' Labour's manifesto by vetoing numerous policies passed by overwhelming majorities at conference. In so doing he further aroused the anger of the left and stored up trouble for the leadership after Labour left office (4.14).

Chapter five deals with the traumatic period between the elections of 1979 and 1983, when Labour underwent virtual civil war. Ex-ministers blamed the unions for all their woes in power (5.1). The rest of the Party disagreed. Most activists were disenchanted with a leadership which, whilst holding office, had ignored conference decisions. The case for making the PLP more accountable to the rest of Party was, it seemed, unanswerable (5.2–4). The position in a number of inner-city CLPs echoed that of the Party as a whole. Once elected, MPs were almost impossible to replace no matter how much they antagonised their members (5.5). For a time, an alliance of activists and certain trade unions carried all before them at conference. Members of this alliance assumed that a more vigorous commitment to 'socialism' – expected to follow increased accountability – would meet with success at the polls (5.6). As some inner-city members believed, Labour could revive its fortunes by becoming the Party of the dispossessed rather than chasing after affluent voters (5.7). The PLP resisted attempts to reduce its influence but was unable to stem the tide. In 1980 the former Bevanite Michael Foot became leader. Despite his past support for internal democracy and policies such as unilateralism, Foot opposed most conference reforms. He and others mistrusted the intentions of Tony Benn, who led this activist revolt, and defended the right of MPs to remain independent of their parties (5.8). In 1981 many of Gaitskell's former supporters left to form the Social Democratic Party (SDP). Constitutional changes that weakened their power and conference support for policies they opposed, allied to their developing hostility to state collectivism and trade union influence within the Party, made their departure almost inevitable (5.9, 5.10). Labour's civil war climaxed during the summer of 1981, when Tony Benn attempted to become deputy leader. Despite Foot's open opposition, Benn came within a whisker of defeating the incumbent, Denis Healey. Some considered that by now the Party's preoccupation with its own internal affairs had fatally damaged its future prospects. Indeed, the contest left the Party more divided than ever (5.11, 5.12). Labour went into the 1983 general election unable to agree on most of its key policies, which were, in any case, unpopular with a large number of voters. It went down to its worst defeat since 1918.

Chapter six covers the period of Neil Kinnock's leadership, in which he attempted to rebuild the Party as an electoral force. Some members considered 1983 a victory of sorts, because Labour's manifesto had at least been 'socialist' (6.1). Kinnock, elected as Foot's successor within months of the election, held no such opinion. To his mind, the result was an unmitigated disaster, which showed that Labour needed to get back in touch with the concerns of ordinary voters (6.2, 6.3). Kinnock's main task, as he saw it, was to reduce the influence of Benn's supporters within the Party and convince others of the need to change key policies (6.4). During this period he also attacked the influence Militant Tendency and expelled its leaders. By no means all approved of his strategy (6.5, 6.6). The defeat of 1987, however, propelled Labour under Kinnock to distance itself ever further from its 1983 programme in the hope that such 'modernisation' would make the Party more popular. Affluent trade unionists, many of whom had voted Conservative since 1979, were a particular target (6.7). By now, even former Bennites recognised the need to appeal to the well off (6.8). Others in the Party called for a fundamental change to the Party's culture (6.9). Marginalised by Kinnock, what was now being described as the 'hard' left was increasingly demoralised and declining in number (6.10). Kinnock's Policy Review, which he hoped would make important strides towards making Labour 'acceptable', could not be stopped. This was despite the Policy Review's emphasis on markets and individualism, which some took to be too close an echo of Margaret Thatcher's rhetoric (6.11, 6.12). Facing a

Conservative government in the midst of a recession, Labour entered the 1992 general election campaign with high hopes. The Party, however, failed to win power under even these auspicious circumstances. Some considered the way the Party handled taxation to have been the main cause of defeat (6.13). Those on the 'hard' left blamed it on Kinnock's reforms, which, they suggested, had made the Party almost indistinguishable from the Conservatives and so gave voters no real reason to vote Labour (6.14).

Despite this fourth successive defeat, as chapter seven shows, there was no question of changing direction. John Smith, Kinnock's successor, may have been cautious, but he had no intention of reversing his predecessor's reforms (7.1). By now most of those on the 'soft' left accepted the need to take full account of individualism (7.2). Smith's death in May 1994 led to the election of Tony Blair, an enthusiastic 'moderniser'. Blair forcefully distanced himself from Labour's past state collectivism (7.3). Although he talked of 'social-ism' few on the left thought he meant much by it, especially as he wanted to do what Gaitskell had failed to accomplish – change clause iv (7.4). Despite some misgivings, Labour members did as Blair wished and replaced the formal commitment to extend public ownership with a form of words deemed more appropriate to 1990s Britain (7.5). Blair supporters saw this as only the beginning of changing Labour into New Labour (7.6). Yet, opposition to the thrust of policy remained and Blair came under pressure to commit himself to full employment and a specific figure for a minimum wage (7.7). There was also disquiet that Blair wished to turn the Party into something wholly alien to its traditions (7.8). Whilst not conceding anything to his critics, Blair emphasised the need for continued change but also stressed the continuity of purpose he enjoyed with his predecessors. Labour under his leadership, Blair claimed, was still concerned to overcome injustice and unfairness even if the policies now stressed the market rather than the state, the individual rather than the collective (7.9).

V

How have historians and political scientists explained Labour's electoral difficulties and assessed the Party's response? The first point to note is the extent to which much of the literature devoted to this subject reflects positions held within the Labour Party itself. Many who have written about the Party have done so as interested observers: a number have been members or former members. Others have occupied antagonistic political positions, invariably to Labour's left. Therefore, the sound of grinding axes is almost deafening when reading most studies of the Party. Whilst partisanship must be taken into account, this should not necessarily invalidate such works. Irrespective of the subject, objectivity is something to which even the most apparently disinterested academic can merely aspire to: it can never be obtained.

There are several explanations of Labour's decline in the literature. Broadly speaking, there is general acceptance that the transformation of British society had *some* negative effect on Labour's fortunes. However, this agreement does not extend to specifying how much of an impact this had on the Party's electoral appeal. One important exception suggests that about half of Labour's decline up to 1983 can be attributed to social change, the other half to specifically political influences.[13] Perhaps on one extreme is Eric Hobsbawm, who has stressed the pre-eminent role played by socio-economic change; on the other is Gareth Stedman Jones, whose emphasis has been on the shortcomings of Labour's political 'language'. Even so, neither author entirely discounts the impact of social or ideological factors.[14] Thus, most analysis converges on the point that Labour made at least *some* contribution to its own decline by the way it responded to social change. Notwithstanding this broad consensus, there is a stark divide between those who consider that the Party's move away from state collectivism accelerated electoral degeneration and those who assert that its cause lies with the fact that such a move occurred all too slowly.

One of the more influential approaches to Labour is motivated by outright hostility to the Party, in particular the parliamentary leadership, due to its alleged ideological shortcomings. Works written within this tradition do not directly address Labour's decline – in part because they were mostly written before it became so acute. They nevertheless offer clear, if implicit, lines of argument. Ralph Miliband's much reprinted *Parliamentary Socialism* is the key text here, but elements of his case are found in works by various later authorities.[15] Miliband wrote to persuade readers that Labour had never been 'socialist' (as he understood the term) and was not capable of becoming such. It was, he wrote in the early 1970s, 'a party of modest social reform in a capitalist system within whose confines it is ever more firmly and by now irrevocably rooted'.[16]

Writers in this tradition usually see the years after 1951 as a kind of fall from grace. Despite its various shortcomings, Labour in the 1940s had happened upon the appropriate policies and thereby acquired an unprecedented level of support. According to John Saville, by moving away from state collectivism in the 1950s Labour entered what he describes as the 'wasted years'. Thus, the leadership 'slowly but inexorably fragmented the diffuse radical consciousness' that had given the Party such appeal in the 1940s.[17] Subsequently, Labour in power dampened down trade union aspirations through the leadership's attempt to maintain capitalism rather than build 'socialism'. Instead of supporting workers in industrial struggle, Labour ministers tried to limit wages and prevent strikes. Wilson and Callaghan alienated the Party's 'natural' supporters, leaving them susceptible to rival Conservative arguments. If only Labour in office had represented workers' demands, all would have been well. As Miliband wrote of the 1964–70 Labour government: it 'could have had all the support it required from trade unionists, had it been seen to be genuinely engaged in the creation of a society marked by greater social justice'. Yet, the leaders were not interested in such an approach. As Miliband wrote in the early 1980s, Labour's leadership did not even stand for 'a "moderate" version of socialism: they stand for a capitalist alternative to it'.[18]

Furthermore, according to Miliband, whilst the leadership failed to give trade unionists a positive reason to vote Labour, they were also unable to attract many 'floating voters'. This latter ambition was, in any case, self-defeating: the more the leadership moderated its programme to appeal to electors on the 'middle ground', the more intolerant such voters became of state collectivism and so the further the leadership had to revise policy in order to win their support.[19] This line of argument has been recently resuscitated by some who have studied Neil Kinnock's Policy Review. According to Eric Shaw, Kinnock's strategy of avoiding offence to affluent voters' sensibilities prevented Labour challenging many Conservative arguments. Instead of trying to change minds, Kinnock accommodated Labour to existing opinions which mistrusted state intervention and deprecated tax increases to pay for welfare. Consequently, in 1992 Labour offered voters no compelling reason to abandon their Conservative loyalties.[20] Thus, it would be fair to suggest that those working within this analytic framework consider that the leadership's lack of commitment to 'socialism' contributed to the Party's electoral troubles; their response to decline merely exacerbated matters.

In contrast to the above is a developing school of thought which suggests that Labour's relatively inflexible response to social change was the prime cause of decline.[21] Significantly, works which propound this view have mainly been written in the wake of Labour's 1983 defeat. Such accounts tend to see the Party's problems as arising from various internal factors and highlight, amongst other things, shortcomings in ideology, organisation and performance in office.[22] Most, however, focus on Labour's ideology and culture. Some have pointed to the 'exhaustion' of the leadership's revisionism and its failure to develop along with circumstances.[23] However, criticism is not restricted to the leadership alone: Party members – activists pre-eminently – are also deemed to have been culpable. Their hostility to changes after 1951, such as the rise of supermarkets, the creation of commercial television and the development of youth culture, betrayed a moralism which rejected the realities of working-class affluence.[24] The contrast with the Conservatives is striking: whilst Labour members despaired of increasing private home ownership amongst the working class, Conservatives embraced it as validating their conception of a 'property-owning democracy'. Thus, by the 1980s, the Conservatives had largely captured the votes of home owners. Yet, the possession of a mortgage does not have an automatic political consequence. It was Labour's earlier high-handed rejection of this ever-increasing phenomenon which defined it as somehow anti-'socialist'; the response of many home owners was, therefore, not surprising.

The focus of most work on the Labour Party after 1951 – whatever the analytic framework – is on national events. This partly reflects the assumption that elections are decided by centrally controlled campaigns. This belief has, however, been recently challenged by the suggestion that local Party members can play a decisive role in the result.[25] Despite this and the work of past political scientists, few historians have taken up the challenge.[26] Such research might reveal much about the character of the Party on the ground and thereby explain why it did so badly. Significantly, one of the few local investigations, that of Labour in Coventry during the 1950s, concluded that the Party was 'narrowly socially based and inward looking', owing to its membership being mainly drawn from local trade union activists. The key to Labour's faltering fortunes in the city was found in this fact; moreover, in being unable to come to terms with social change the Party was 'a victim of its own ideology and traditions'.[27]

This latter approach stresses, to a greater or lesser extent, the consequences of Labour's failure to develop an appropriate political 'language' to meet the demands of changing social conditions. Instead of innovating, Labour has been accused of looking back to the period 1945–51, described in the early 1980s by Gareth Stedman Jones as 'a magical moment to which all sections of the party have yearned to return'.[28] Moreover, recent work suggests that, during this 'magical moment', Labour's support was less firm and less principled than some have believed.[29] Thus, in harking back to the past, many in the Party deluded themselves about its real character.

Those who have written about the Policy Review also differ over how best to describe its impact on the Party's ideological character. According to some, Labour by the 1990s had adopted an 'ersatz Thatcherism'; others have suggested that Labour had reverted to positions adopted by the Edwardian Liberal Party. Broadly speaking, the Review is seen by many as constituting the leadership's final rejection of 'socialism' in the belief that this would improve Labour's chances at the polls.[30] Eric Shaw has even described the Review as 'post-revisionist'. According to him, Kinnock had abandoned even Anthony Crosland's revisionist programme by adopting policies which favoured capitalism at the expense of those which protected workers.[31]

Others, most prominently Martin J. Smith, have suggested that it would be more accurate to see the Review as a return to Crosland's revisionism rather than a departure from it. In essence, he thinks Kinnock's changes were consistent with the perspective adopted by Crosland, Gaitskell and, in effect, all Labour leaders since 1951. The parliamentary leadership had always thought of 'socialism' as a form of capitalism in which the state played a limited but important role: in this 'socialism' the free market had limits placed on its influence but still played a central role in the economy. This viewpoint suggests that those who think Labour abandoned 'socialism' under Kinnock do so on the basis of a definition of 'socialism' never accepted by the leadership. If there was a departure from traditional perspectives, it did not occur in the late 1980s but at the start of that decade, when the Party adopted a range of unprecedentedly left-wing policies.[32]

To some extent, Smith's analysis echoes that of Miliband: Labour was never 'socialist' if by that is meant the transcendence of capitalism and placing the interests of the organised working class at the centre of policy. However, he draws the opposite conclusion: that Labour's adherence to such a 'socialism' was not the route to electoral success but, instead, oblivion. Such a discussion raises the question: how profitable is it to talk of Labour's 'socialism' given the existence of so many divergent definitions of the term within the Party? Both Gaitskell and Kinnock described themselves as 'socialists' whilst Tony Blair has announced his adherence to 'social-ism'. Yet, these leaders have been opposed by those who similarly believed themselves 'socialists'. Thus, protagonists who battle over what they consider to be Labour's traditional adherence to 'socialism' might benefit from one description of the Party as 'a perpetually shifting fulcrum between contending ... pressures' from both the left and right.[33] In other words, the suggestion is, there has never been an essential Labour view about the character of 'socialism'.

One final point about the literature: if there have been few local accounts of the Labour Party during this period, there have been too few comparative studies which place Labour's problems in a wider European context. The lack of comparative work is remarkable, as such work can only help identify common and distinct causes, thereby clarifying and perhaps challenging much of the analysis outlined above.[34]

VI

This collection's main purpose is to illustrate how the Labour Party interpreted and then responded to its electoral predicament.

Consequently, it contains only documents generated by the Labour Party, its officers, members and former members. Notwithstanding the relatively narrow range of possible sources used, the documents include: local Party newsletters, political tracts, journal and newspaper articles, Party reports, manifestos, transcripts of speeches, a novel, memoirs, autobiographies, local party minutes, NEC minutes, diaries and private correspondence. This is no mean list.

As might be expected, the balance of published and un-published sources tilts substantially in favour of the former as the period proceeds. No records generated by the Labour govern-ments have been consulted owing to the rule which prevents the release of state material for thirty years. The national Labour Party also prohibits any of its internal material being consulted until ten years have elapsed. Some CLPs have similar pro-hibitions. However, the real problem with local party records of any nature is that relatively few have been deposited either with their local libraries or with county record offices. Of those papers so deposited, few have material relevant to the period after 1970 and hardly any to the years after 1980.

Whilst local records have been rather neglected by historians, those generated by the parliamentary leadership – in particular the autobiographies and diaries of leading participants – are more regularly quoted. The temptation to over-exploit diaries is especially strong. The likes of Richard Crossman, Barbara Castle and Tony Benn and – to a much lesser extent – Hugh Gaitskell and Patrick Gordon Walker – were both important figures and interesting diarists. Taken together they give the historian an unequalled insight into the thinking of prominent figures during the 1950s, 1960s and 1970s. Benn's published diaries are unique in that they cover the entire period; he is also much the most significant figure to keep a diary. Yet, as Benn himself has noted, perhaps a little harshly:

> The trouble about a personal diary is that it is entirely subjective. It is not history, nor has it any value except such as it gets from the personal slant on events. But of course these events are the framework on which the thin personal story is woven. Every now and again one has to step back a little and assess the changes that are taking place outside.[35]

At least diaries do not have the 'advantage' of hindsight. Benn's in particular reveal his developing perspective in response to events. Autobiographies are, for this reason, of less use, as they are based on the (usually recently retired) politician's urge to defend her or his record. Some exceptions apart, candour is often conspicuous by its absence.

The student of the contemporary Labour Party must await the availability of a fuller range of possible sources. Retirement and death will increase access to private papers. Distance should also make participants – major and minor – more willing to tell that bit of the 'truth' they can recall. Yet, the sources already on offer give a very detailed picture of the Party. Lack of documentary evidence is not the real problem: as ever, a source is only as good as the person interpreting it.

1

Interpreting defeat, 1951–59

Despite losing the 1951 general election, most Labour Party members were confident that, after a brief and disastrous period of Conservative rule, Labour would return to power. There was less certainty about which direction Labour would follow once back in office. Activists and those MPs who supported the former minister Aneurin Bevan wanted to increase state control of the economy. They saw this as a prerequisite for 'socialism'. Others, most prominently Clement Attlee, major trade union leaders and the overwhelming majority of MPs, considered it expedient to consolidate. They thought extending the state's economic role would alienate key voters. This latter view prevailed. Even so, the leadership's moderation found no electoral reward: Labour lost the general election of 1955. Despite this, Hugh Gaitskell, elected leader after that defeat, sought to reduce further the Party's association with nationalisation.

1.1 Labour's 'moral victory'

Whilst Labour won fewer seats than the Conservatives in 1951, the Party actually gained more votes. Consequently, most members refused to view the result as a defeat. This attitude is reflected in comments contained in a monthly paper produced by the Labour Party in Essex.

A glance at the national general election results reveals at once that Labour has no cause to be either ashamed or disheartened....

The Tories, with only a precarious majority, have now to govern this country. They are faced with a hopeless dilemma. They have to carry through a representative Conservative policy, which their wealthy backers will expect, of cutting social services, lowering taxation and reinstating class privileges; and at the same time they must try to make some show of carrying their explicit but impossible promises to maintain Labour's social reforms and services, to build up to 300,000 houses and to lower the cost of living – they must contrive to be both pink and blue!

We do not believe that they had ever the least intention to operate any of their pledges, which were for election purposes only. Such aims are mutually contradictory and cannot be achieved. It is only a question of time – and probably only a short time – before the hollowness of Tory pretences is exposed. Then will our people be glad to return to the Socialist planning now interrupted, which has saved and revived this country, and will turn again with relief to the policy of social justice which is implicit in Labour's principles, and of which Toryism knows nothing.

The Labour Party can be trusted to fight hard in Parliament. Our task in the constituencies now is to keep up and improve our organisation and our propaganda; to be always ready for 'the Day', which cannot be long deferred. This Tory night can only be brief, and though the Tories will inevitably do some mischief, they cannot reverse the march of social progress. With the first light of dawn, they and their misdeeds will vanish.

Labour Party Archive, Manchester (hereafter LPA), *Romford, Hornchurch & Brentwood Labour Voice*, mid-November 1951.

1.2 The future is secure

Whilst more measured in their analysis, those in the Party's highest echelons also responded to defeat with some optimism. Morgan Phillips, Labour's general secretary, here reflects on the lessons of 1951.

One of the outstanding features of the Campaign was the personal success of Clement Attlee wherever he went during his election tour. Some of his audiences were as large as 15,000 but no matter how large or small the gathering, his appearance was the occasion for moving and appreciative demonstrations of affection and loyalty....

The Party is in good fettle. It enjoys increasing support in the country despite the heavy barrage of misrepresentation and the whispering campaigns to which it has been subjected during the past six and a half years. At the same time, we cannot overlook the fact that Labour's poll of 48.7 per cent of all votes cast, only represents 40 per cent of the total electorate. And it is to the remaining 60 per cent of whom many are trade unionists and their wives that we must look for future victories.

We must begin now to raise our individual membership, to improve our financial position locally and nationally, to appoint more full-time agents, and to intensify our propaganda and educational activities so that our people are better equipped to counter Tory misrepresentation. Given the effort, the will and the determination, we can be confident that final victory for democratic socialism is assured.

LPA, NEC minutes, 7 November 1951, Morgan Phillips, 'General Election Campaign 1951. General Secretary's Report' (not dated), p. 6.

1.3   Maintaining the faith

During the early period of opposition it seemed to many activists that the route back to power was guaranteed, so long as members remained true to Labour's original purpose. This editorial from a Labour monthly paper, distributed in the Reigate constituency in Surrey, describes adherence to the 'socialist' faith as crucial.

It is a common experience in history that enthusiasm and zeal thrive on adversity. The early Christians were prepared to suffer hardship and even martyrdom for their faith, whereas the average Christian of to-day, if he has the good fortune to live in a country where freedom and tolerance are the rule, is at best lukewarm in his enthusiasm for his faith....

So it is with our Labour movement. The hardy pioneers in the early part of the century struggled hard against what appeared to be overwhelming odds to secure the return to Parliament of a handful of Labour Members, and the amount of effort expended in what would have seemed to us a hopeless task, only stirred them to still greater endeavours at immense personal sacrifice.

Now that Labour has won its position as the greatest political force in the country, considerable numbers of the workers seem content to sit back complacently and enjoy the position which has been won.

We should do well to remember that nothing can ever be static. Our movement must be either forwards or backwards, and unless we can revive some of the old enthusiasm of the early pioneers, it will be backwards.

Nor is it any use leaving the enthusiasm to others on the grounds such as that we are too busy, not entirely in agreement with the policy of the Party on certain matters, and so on. Each individual member of the Party matters and the whole is made up of the individual members. Having won so much, perhaps we take it for granted, and just as hardship stimulated effort, so our present happier conditions, won by the struggles of those early pioneers, seem to breed indolence.

If we want to keep what we have won and to win even more, we must be prepared for a little self-sacrifice. AND THIS MEANS YOU – NOT THE OTHER MAN.

LPA, *Reigate Constituency Clarion*, August 1952.

1.4   Uncertain direction

> Others were less sure that the future was so clearly mapped out. They doubted that members merely had to renew their faith in 'socialism' to ensure the re-election of a Labour government. In fact, during the last days of the Attlee administration a few had detected a worrying lack of direction. Perhaps, they suggested, the Party needed to revise some of its policies. The Coventry MP Richard Crossman[1] was one such sceptic.

Even before the 1950 election, the impetus which brought the Labour Government to power began to fail. That impetus, despite a sharp setback in 1931, had mounted steadily during the fifty years of opposition – years spent in a sustained campaign against the capitalist order. Yet, after scarcely four years in office, the Government had fulfilled its historic mission. The nationalisation of half a dozen major industries, the construction of an all-in system of social security and a free health service, and a tentative application of planning to the national economy – the achievement of these reforms seemed to have exhausted the content of British socialism.

What was the cause of this loss of political momentum? Not the deadlock result of the 1950 election – far less the need for rearmament after the attack on South Korea. Even if the Labour Government in 1950 had won a large parliamentary majority, the advance to socialism would have been halted. The right wing openly advocated consolidation; the left demanded more socialism, but could only suggest those measures required to achieve it. The rearmament programme (and the defeat in the polls in 1951) came as a deliverance from indecision, not an obstacle to action.

It would be easy to attribute this indecision to a failure of leadership. Certainly, the almost simultaneous loss of his two strong men, Sir Stafford Cripps and Mr. Bevin,[2] grievously weakened the Prime Minister's position and revealed a dangerous rift in his Cabinet. But these personal factors were symptoms of a much more serious ailment, a failure of the sense of direction which alone can unify and sustain a great political party. The Labour Party was unsure where it was going. The familiar landmarks on the road to socialism had been left behind: it was travelling in a strange country, exposed to climatic rigours it had not anticipated and against which its traditional equipment gave little protection. Buffeted and battered, it pushed ahead; but the pace had slowed as it became clear that the destination would not be reached by the traditional route.

R. H. S. Crossman, 'Towards a philosophy of socialism', in R. H. S. Crossman (ed.), *New Fabian Essays*, London, 1952, pp. 1–2.

1.5   How to win: the Gaitskellite formula

If Labour had achieved a moral victory in 1951, it still needed to win more votes. Those sympathetic to Hugh Gaitskell, seen as a potential leader since becoming Chancellor of the Exchequer in 1950, considered that Labour had to appeal to 'floating voters'. By this they essentially meant the middle class. As the monthly journal *Socialist Commentary* indicated, this implied changing a number of policies which many members held dear.

The picture which has been emerging since the war, and which has been confirmed by this election ... is this. The Labour and Tory parties face each other in fairly even strength. Both are supported by large blocs of voters who possess an extraordinary and virtually unshakeable loyalty. There is no extreme right or left wing of even potential strength, and no alternative 'centre'.... For both the big parties the field of operation in which to win new support, at least in the immediate future, has been narrowed almost out of existence.... Both parties have gradually been pushed further towards the centre. The battle for the floating vote – which fluctuates somewhere in the centre, or in the case of non-voters is stationary there – remains as the only method of changing the parliamentary position, unsatisfactory as it is for both parties.

... The glaring grievances of the past have, through our own efforts, been eliminated. Through public controls, social services and the redistribution of income, we have at least the beginnings of an egalitarian society and although no one pretends that the whole job has been done, we must look beyond the old gospel of more and more nationalisation, 'workers' control' or class appeals to 'soak the rich'.

... Up till now, we have been engrossed in securing a decent material basis of life, and a sense of social security for every citizen, and that was the natural and urgent first priority when so many people lived on or below the poverty line. They do so no longer, and socialists must now devote at least part of their efforts to examining what is needed for creating not only an equal society, but a good and rich one.

Editorial, *Socialist Commentary*, 11:11, November 1951, pp. 246–7.

1.6   How to win: the Bevanite formula

In contrast to *Socialist Commentary*'s schema, Bevan's supporters wanted a renewed emphasis on nationalisation. After reading Gallup's survey of opinion at the 1951 general election, Bevanite MP Geoffrey Bing concluded that a promise to extend state control of the economy would detach

sufficient working-class support from the Conservatives to
guarantee Labour's return to power.

It is reasonable to suppose that on the one hand, the seats where
Labour has the best chance of making progress are those where
the Tories rely to the largest extent on a working class vote. On
the other hand, it is fair to assume that the higher the degree of
trade union organisation the smaller will be the proportion of the
working class who vote Tory. In other words the Tories are most
vulnerable in those constituencies which are least organised
industrially, because these contain a greater proportion of
potential converts. Yet these are often the most marginal of Tory
seats. A deviation of a comparatively small percentage of the Tory
working class vote might not affect very materially the overall
total vote, but might result in a significant swing in seats in the
House [of Commons].

... The Labour vote at the last election is calculated to be 91
per cent working class and 9 per cent middle class. The Tory vote
is calculated at 40 per cent well-to-do and middle class and 60
per cent working class. This working class Tory vote includes 12
per cent of the very poor and 15 per cent of trade union
members. So Labour could well afford to sacrifice every single
middle class vote if it could secure even two-thirds of the Tory
trade unionists....

The Tories could be out of power for ever by [Labour] winning
over as little as one-fifth of the present working class support that
they receive. This alone would reduce their poll by 12 per cent
and thus their seats in the House to under 150.

Two things are necessary to achieve this – a strong campaign
before the election and a clear, simple Socialist policy. The
confusion of mind of the electors which the [Gallup] Poll reveals
is to a large degree merely a reflection of the confusion into
which we have allowed our own policy to fall.

Tribune, 28 December 1951.

1.7 Bevan's beliefs

Aneurin Bevan articulated ideas and sentiments which
echoed those of many activists. Even after his death in 1960

Bevan remained a much-quoted figure on the left: Neil Kinnock often referred to him, at least during his early period as leader. What follows is a selection of Bevan's thoughts on a number of central topics, taken from his personal manifesto *In Place of Fear*, first published in 1952.

1.7(a) The British constitution

Whilst Bevan differed with Attlee's shadow cabinet over economic policy, he was in accord with them in believing that Parliament was the only appropriate means of political advance. Indeed, such was Bevan's constitutional conservatism that he even opposed reforming the House of Lords. This lack of interest in constitutional change remained general throughout the Party until the later 1970s.

The absence of a written constitution gives British politics a flexibility enjoyed by few nations. No courts can construe the power of the British Parliament. It interprets its own authority, and from it there is no appeal. This gives it a revolutionary quality, and enables us to entertain the hope of bringing about social transformations, without the agony and prolonged crises experienced by less fortunate nations. The British constitution, with its adult suffrage, exposes all rights and privileges, properties and powers, to the popular will. The only checks are those that arise from a sense of justice and social propriety. Thus, in the Parliament of 1945–50, a large section of the economic apparatus was transferred from private to public ownership on terms which were admittedly generous: too generous, some thought. But the transfer was made smoothly, peacefully and with political decorum.... Our present political institutions are adequate for all our purposes.

1.7(b) The need for 'principle'

Those on the Labour left have been referred to as the keepers of the Party's 'conscience'. This sense of moral superiority over the more pragmatic leadership is clearly evident in Bevan. According to him, Labour needed to stick to its principles and not try to placate the electorate's passing mood.

It is the practice of many publicists to sneer at the Labour Party for clinging to what are called 'doctrinaire' principles. You would imagine from the manner of these attacks that lack of principle is a suitable political equipment [*sic*]. No statesman can stand the strain of modern political life without the inner serenity that comes from fidelity to a number of guiding convictions. Without their steadying influence he is blown about by every passing breeze. Nor is cleverness and political agility a substitute for them. It has always been for me a painful spectacle when some Labour spokesman tries to justify a piece of Socialist legislation on exclusively 'practical' grounds. There are at least two considerations to be kept in mind when making policy. Its applicability to the immediate situation certainly; but also its faithfulness to the general body of principles which make up your philosophy. Without the latter, politics is merely a job like any other.

... Then there is the disposition to smooth away the edges of policy in the hope of making it more attractive to doubtful supporters. It is better to risk a clear and definite rejection than to win uneasy followers by dexterous ambiguities.

Whenever the Labour Party has made a mistake, it has not been in consequence of pursuing its principles too roughly or too far, but by making too many concessions to conventional opinion.

1.7(c) The case for nationalisation

One of the principles most firmly adhered to by Bevan was the need to extend Labour's nationalisation programme. This, he considered, lay at the heart of 'socialism'.

... judged from any angle, the relations between public and private enterprise have not yet reached a condition where they can be stabilised. That is why it is so foolish for certain Labour men to preach 'consolidation' at this stage. Before we can dream of consolidation, the power relations of public and private property must be drastically altered....

35

That is not to say a halting place cannot be reached. I think it can. It is clear to the serious student of modern politics that a mixed economy is what most people in the West would prefer. The victory of Socialism need not be universal to be decisive.... It is neither prudent, nor does it accord with our conception of the future, that all forms of private property should live under perpetual threat. In almost all types of human society different forms of property have lived side by side without fatal consequences for society or for one of them. But it is a requisite of social stability that one type of property ownership should dominate. In the society of the future it should be public property. Private property should yield to the point where social purposes and a decent order of priorities form an easily discernible pattern of life. Only when this is accomplished will a tranquil and serene attitude take the place of the all-pervading restlessness that is the normal climate of competitive society....

In the Western world the extension of the principles of public ownership will be influenced by the extent to which large aggregations of private capital have coagulated into monopolies and semi-monopolies in which profit is a clear tax on the community and no longer a reward for risk.

1.7(d)   Nationalisation's wider purpose

Nationalisation was not conceived in purely economic terms. It also held the key to change in social relationships. From this extract, the extent to which Bevan's support for nationalisation was motivated by moral and democratic concerns is made clear.

The conversion of an industry to public ownership is only the first step towards Socialism. It is an all-important step, for without it the conditions of further progress are not established.... The advance from State ownership to full Socialism is in direct proportion to the extent the workers in the nationalised sector are made aware of a changed relationship between themselves and the management. The persistence of a sense of dualism in a publicly owned industry is evidence of an immature industrial democracy. It means that emotionally the 'management' is still associated with the conception of alien ownership, and the 'workers' are still the 'hands'.

Until we make the cross-over to a spirit of co-operation, the latent energies of democratic participation cannot be fully released; nor shall we witness that spiritual homogeneity which comes when the workman is united once more with the tools of his craft, a unity which was ruptured by the rise of economic classes. The individual citizen will still feel that society is on top of him until he is enfranchised in the workshop as well as at the ballot box.

Aneurin Bevan, *In Place of Fear*, London, 1952, (a) pp. 100–2, (b) pp. 96–7, (c) pp. 118–19, (d) pp. 102–3.

1.8   A divided party

> Hostility to Bevan's ideas and anger at his occasional habit of not following the Labour whip in Parliament caused Hugh Gaitskell to lead an ultimately futile attempt to expel Bevan from the PLP. At the same time Labour prepared for the forthcoming 1955 general election by holding a number of pre-campaign rallies. At one such meeting Gaitskell spoke; as he recorded in his diary, it was quite eventful.

It had been arranged that I should speak in Wolverhampton, supported by Baird, a completely mad and unpleasant Bevanite, and Stanley Evans, who is on the extreme right of the Party.[3] The attendance was middling. It was a good hall, and about half or two-thirds full. Stanley was going to take no chances with Baird, and at once launched a great attack on Mr B[evan].... He was, of course, heavily heckled, but took no notice. Baird then got up and replied in kind. I think this was slightly comic for a 'Forward to Victory' demonstration. He ended with an appeal to me to say that night that I was against the expulsion of Mr Bevan. I refused, however, to say anything on this, and after replying to the more extravagant statements which Baird had made on foreign policy – clear all the Americans out of Europe, etc. – I proceeded to try and bring the meeting round to its real purpose, and did my usual Home Front stuff. There were about 20 Communists, and about half the rest were Bevanites. It all ended reasonably happily, but it was a reckless idea to put the three of us on the same platform. Fortunately, though, the newspaper strike is on, and only the local papers reported what took place.

Philip M. Williams (ed.), *The Diary of Hugh Gaitskell, 1945–1956*, London, 1983: entry for 2 April 1955, pp. 396–7.

1.9   An 'affluent society'?

> Despite the leadership's later claim, Bevanite dissension was not responsible for Labour's 1955 defeat. The Conservatives had adapted most of Labour's state collectivist policies to suit their own purposes and enjoyed the political consequences of economic growth. As is clear from this extract from the diary of Hugh Dalton, senior Labour figures like himself considered that what would be later termed the 'affluent society' had won the election for the Conservatives well before the campaign had even begun.

Kenneth Younger[4] came to see me in the flat.... We agreed that the Tories would win seats at a general election now. We had no attractive programme. People were content with the Tories. They had stolen the Socialists' clothes (full employment; welfare state, etc.). I said it must be disappointing to him, and others of his age, young ex-ministers, to have the prospect of waiting another six years for office. He said No. He didn't want it at present, or till the Party knew better what *it* wanted, and there was a much better spirit.

I spoke of the much more intense interest taken by many young people in Africans, Indians, etc. He said, very truly, that, having done away with gross poverty, extremes of wealth here, this was where the emotions now went, and the moral indignation, that used to find a natural vent at home. I said that, when I first went to Bishop Auckland as prospective candidate in 1928, and met leading members of the Party, they were nearly all unemployed miners, shabby and hungry. Last month they were in evening dress (not optional), yes, including some miners, at Civic Dinner of Labour controlled Council [*sic*].

Ben Pimlott (ed.), *The Political Diary of Hugh Dalton, 1918–40, 1945–60*, London, 1986: entry for 24 March 1955, pp. 620–1.

1.10   A 'corrupt' society?

Not all agreed with Dalton. Some thought the economy still promoted inequalities whilst it tempted the people with corrupt values. George Rogers, MP for the London constituency of north Kensington, reminded his CLP of the need to retain their faith in nationalisation.

The Tories have undone much that we did during our six years of office. Selfish individualism has again been given the green light: profits soar, price-fixing cartels grow, shoddy goods make their reappearance and we return to the 'Boom and Slump' economy that caused so much misery in the past. The corrupting influence of commercialism gains new ground with the introduction of advertising in the powerful medium of television. Transport has been plunged into chaos. All these must be put right and we must go forward to the new Socialist reorganisation so that the standards of the people can be raised.... They say that nationalisation does not work. Every bonny child that we see around us gives them the lie for it is the national health service that has made available to all treatment and services that were formerly and regularly obtained by the rich. Yes, it is indeed national enterprise that is responsible for the fine generation of children of whom we are so proud. We must go on until all things are available for all men.

British Library of Political and Economic Science Archives, London School of Economics (hereafter BLPES), North Kensington Labour Party papers, *North Kensington Labour Quarterly*, April (?) 1955.

1.11   The 'penny-farthing' machine

One explanation of defeat, which gained currency in 1955, was the inferiority of Labour's organisation compared with that of the Conservatives. Under Harold Wilson a team drawn from the NEC investigated the subject. They delivered a damning report which detailed the extent of inefficiency within the Party's organisation. Despite this, little was done to remedy the situation in later years – in particular under the leadership of Wilson himself.

After what we have seen of the Party organisation throughout the country our surprise is not that the General Election was lost, but that we won as many seats as we did. We were particularly disturbed by what appears to be the progressive deterioration of the Party's organisation, especially at constituency level. Constituencies which were not particularly well organised in 1950 and 1951 have declined seriously since then, and, at a time when our opponents' organisation has been becoming more streamlined and efficient, ours has been getting worse....

We have not as a Sub-committee been holding an inquest into our electoral defeat; that would involve questions far wider than Party organisation. Obviously full employment, overtime and the widespread employment of married women affected not only our political attitudes but also the numbers of voluntary workers willing and able to carry on election activities. Apathy, disputes in the Party, national and local, the absence of sufficient clearly defined differences between the parties, disillusionment with nationalisation in the way it has been presented to the public, the rationing scare: all these have played their part. The main effect of all this has been to reduce the numbers and enthusiasm of Party workers available. With the exception of a small number of constituencies, mainly marginal, all reports have confirmed that voluntary workers were fewer and less enthusiastic than at any previous time. Many of those who did work for a Labour victory were older men and women: with many it was habit rather than enthusiasm which provided the motive force....

We do not wish to give the impression that every constituency was ... badly organised.... In many constituencies, especially marginal seats where a keen contest was fought, efficient organisation and fighting enthusiasm went hand in hand. But the fact remains that compared to our opponents, we are still at the penny-farthing stage in a jet-propelled era, and our machine, at that, is getting rusty and deteriorating with age.

'Interim Report of the Sub-Committee on Party Organisation', *Labour Party Annual Conference Report 1955*, London, 1955, pp. 64–5.

1.12   Crosland's revisionism

Gaitskell's leadership was defined by his attempt to move the Party away from its identification with nationalisation. Anthony Crosland's *The Future of Socialism*, first published in 1956, is usually seen to have provided Gaitskell, a friend of the author, with the intellectual justification for this strategy.[5] In fact, it was but one of a number of works written at about the same time which all made rather similar cases. Crosland, however, made a particularly clear and coherent case for the new leadership's priorities. It was a work which also continued to be cited in the 1980s by the Party's social democrats, such as Roy Hattersley, Kinnock's deputy.

1.12(a)   Capitalism transformed

Crosland's argument was based on his assertion that since the 1930s capitalism had been transformed, largely as a result of the Attlee government's own policies. Here, he calls on Labour to recognise this and adapt its policies accordingly.

Capitalism has been reformed almost out of recognition. Despite occasional minor recessions and balance of payments crises, full employment and at least a tolerable degree of stability are likely to be maintained. Automation can be expected steadily to solve any remaining problems of under-production. Looking ahead, our present rate of growth will give us a national output three times as high now in 50 years – an increase capable of sustaining ... a generous rise in home living standards.... The pre-war reasons for a largely economic orientation [for 'socialism'] are therefore steadily losing their relevance; and we can increasingly divert our energies into more fruitful and idealistic channels, and to fulfilling earlier and more fundamental socialist aspirations.

1.12(b)   The case against further nationalisation

The policy Crosland thought required most revision was
Labour's commitment to increase public ownership. Because
of the new economic conditions identified in his study,
Crosland considered nationalisation irrelevant to the
promotion of equality, which he described as Labour's main
purpose.

The Labour Party having decided, rightly, to pay full compensation, the transfer of industries to state ownership does not
have any large or immediate effect on the distribution of income.
Over the long run there is, of course, a connection; but even in
the long run other methods of redistribution are now seen to be
simpler and more effective. As a determinant of relative shares in
total income, the ownership of industrial property is less
important than the level of employment, the behaviour of prices,
government controls (e.g. over rent or dividends), and above all
taxation policy; and a determined government can restrict
property incomes more easily than by the collectivisation of
industry with full compensation. In addition, nationalisation has
thrown up certain stubborn and largely unexpected problems
which, so long as they remain unsolved, in any case make it
impracticable to rely on public ownership as the main method of
raising wages at the expense of property incomes.

In fact the other methods have already gone some way to
fulfilling the desired objective. There has been an important
transfer from property-incomes to wages since 1939; and the
distribution of wealth is now much more egalitarian. Certainly
much remains to be done; but fiscal policies offer a simpler and
quicker way of doing it than wholesale collectivisation.

This does not mean that nationalisation may not be justified on
other grounds, nor that over the long period it has no influence of
any kind on income-distribution, nor that the egalitarian
objective to which it was directed has lost its relevance. It simply
means that the ownership of the means of production ... is no
longer the essential determinant of the distribution of incomes;
private ownership is compatible with a high degree of equality,
while state ownership, as the Russian experience has demonstrated, may be used to support a high degree of inequality.

1.12(c) The abiding aim of 'socialism'

Having demonstrated that many of Labour's policies were irrelevant to contemporary Britain, Crosland identified those goals which in his opinion should form Labour's purpose in the 1950s and beyond. The most important of these was the active promotion of equality.

Lord Attlee recently remarked, looking back on his early days, that 'I joined the socialist movement because I did not like the kind of society we had and I wanted something better'. Why should anyone say the same to-day?

There are, I believe, three answers. First, for all the rising material standards and apparent contentment, the areas of avoidable social distress and physical squalor ... are still on a scale which narrowly restricts the freedom of choice and movement of large numbers of individuals. Secondly (and perhaps more intractable), we retain a disturbing amount, compared to some other countries, of social antagonism and class resentment, visible both in politics and industry, and making society less peaceful and contented than it might be. Thirdly, the distribution of rewards and privileges still appears highly inequitable, being poorly correlated with the distribution of merit, virtue, ability, or brains; and in particular, opportunities for gaining the top rewards are still excessively unequal.

The significant residue of distress, resentment, and injustice affords a *prima facie* justification for further social change ... in a socialist direction. It may not justify the same *saeva indignatio* as mass unemployment and distressed areas before the war – rather a purposeful, constructive, and discriminating determination to improve an already improved society. But the belief that further change will appreciably increase personal freedom, social contentment, and justice, constitutes the ethical basis for being a socialist.

C. A. R. Crosland, *The Future of Socialism*, London, 1956, (a) p. 517, (b) p. 89, (c) p. 116.

1.13 Christian Socialists and equality

There was another tradition which, in certain parts of the country, had a much greater influence on Party thinking than Crosland's sophisticated arguments. This was Christian Socialism. The Welsh MP Reverend Llewellyn Williams here argues for equality, but on grounds rather different to those advanced by either Bevan or Crosland.

Our forefathers in the Labour Party were, in the main, humble, unknown men and women.

But they had a sense of what was right and proper. They had a vision of a new society to be created, and to that creation they brought the evangelical fervour and spirit of the Christian pioneers who 'had all things common.'

From the mines and factories, from the pulpits and Sunday Schools they went forth persecuted and ridiculed to rouse the conscience of a Christian country which tolerated either through indifference or naked greed, social injustices which made a mockery of Christian teaching.

We seek, with the inspiration and fellowship of our Christian members, representing all denominations, to carry on the task our pioneers entrusted to us. Here is the answer of the Christian Socialist:–

We believe in Equality.

We believe that all the children of God are equal in His love.

And we believe that they should have every possible equality of opportunity to live to the full His priceless gift of life.

Am I my brother's keeper?

Yes, says Labour. And through the programmes we prepare for future Labour governments, we intend to practise what we preach.

The Democrat. All Wales Socialist Monthly, September 1956.

1.14   The call for Party democracy

Whilst many activists criticised Gaitskell's revisionism, they were unable to prevent him de-emphasising the role of nationalisation. With Bevan seeking to make peace with the new leader after 1955, a number on the left gathered around Victory for Socialism (VFS). One of its aims was to reduce the influence of the mainly pro-Gaitskell union block vote at conference and increase members' ability to influence decisions. At the inaugural meeting of VFS, Hugh Jenkins,[6] as chair of the organisation, spoke on behalf of those who did so much for the Party but whose voices were ignored.

We are the people who address the envelopes and deliver them.

We are the people who collect the subscriptions.

We are the people who attend Ward Meetings – who hold the jumble sales and give the children's parties. We take the chair and write the minutes and draw up the agendas and do the canvassing. We are the people who fight hopeless seats. We are the people who knock on the doors. And if anyone wants to know why Labour lost the last election – we can tell them in one sentence without any investigation. *Too many people stopped knocking on doors.* They didn't join the Tories, still less the Communists or any section of the lunatic fringe which nowadays includes the Liberals. They just sat at home and looked at the television. Why? Because they had reached the conclusion that the leadership of the Labour Party had lost faith in socialism and they were not prepared to go on slogging away for a Parliamentary machine which only wanted the use of their feet and hands and frustrated and denied them the fruits of their dreams and their minds and their voices. The great Morrison[7] fallacy had done its work – the fallacy that you have to gear your policy to the floating voter – to aim somewhere in the no-man's land of a dead liberalism which is imagined to lie between Tory and Labour.

The way to win elections is to allow the man who knocks on the doors a voice in deciding policy. To give him something worth knocking on doors about. To remove his frustration and fill him with the enthusiasm to tackle a soul-destroying job.

BLPES, Hugh Jenkins papers, 6/9, Victory for Socialism conference, 7 April 1956, address by Hugh Jenkins.

1.15 Opposition to constitutional change

Gaitskell's supporters saw no need to reduce the voice of the unions and increase that of the members: they were the

block vote's beneficiaries. In a reply to a letter from Hugh
Jenkins, William Rodgers, general secretary of the Fabian
Society – later a cabinet minister and founder of the SDP –
rejected this call for increased democracy. Rodgers would
eventually change his mind when, in the later 1970s, union
leaders were more critical of the leadership.

Of course the dominance of the trade unions and the use of the
block vote at Conference sometimes has undesirable results; and
of course final decisions tend to be made by comparatively few
people who hold the power. In the last five or six years in
particular this has had frustrating effects on occasions. But is it
true that there is an alternative – and one for which support can
be won – that promises better? I doubt it.

The important thing is to keep the trade unions in politics and
on the side of Labour. I'm sure you would agree. After that, what
we must do is to keep them moving and prevent them becoming
ossified: which is a problem with all large-scale organisations. I
believe we will succeed, not by constant criticism of the way they
use their power, but by making them feel at home with the political
wing. The very great mistake the Left can make is to give the
trade unions, which means their leaders, a sense of isolation.
They want to be liked: they even want to be guided. This means a
tactful getting together and not criticism from afar....

So I'm in favour of leaving the constitution alone, at least for
the time being. Those who advocate a change because their
policies have not been adopted under the present structure are in
a weak moral position. It is better to wait till the issues are not so
controversial. Meanwhile, let's have more personal contact
between leading trade unionists and politicians.

BLPES, Hugh Jenkins papers, 6/9, letter from W. T. Rodgers to
Hugh Jenkins, 29 December 1955.

1.16   MPs and their Party

The relationship between MPs and the rest of the Party,
subject to increasing scrutiny in the 1970s and 1980s, was
hardly ideal even in the 1950s. In *No Love for Johnnie*, a
posthumously published novel, the MP William Fienburgh

portrayed one fictional Labour MP's attitude to ordinary
Party workers. The novel also paints an unfavourable view
of some constituency social activities.

The Mayor of Earnley was standing by the station barrier peering
over the ticket collector's shoulders, and the Member of
Parliament spotted him as he stepped down from the train. He
now had the knack of instantaneously recognizing the faceless
local notability sent to meet him. After years of addressing public
meetings, mass demonstrations and week-end schools from
Cornwall to Kent to Argyll, he no longer needed the usual
elaborate identification symbols.

'I shall be wearing a red tie' it had been in the late thirties,
when the political atmosphere had been passionate and
revolutionary. During the war it was 'I shall be carrying a copy of
the *New Statesman*'. This was the badge of the new thinking
which could construct a new post-war world in an hour's
discussion over spam sandwiches and saccharined tea. In the early
fifties they carried *Tribune*. Nowadays they were flattering
enough to write: *I have seen you once or twice on television so
I'm sure I shall recognize you, Yours fraternally, etc.* But he could
always pick them out....

He also knew what they were going to say. 'I'm afraid we
haven't got a big audience for you this time.' So much was
inevitable, but the excuses varied. 'We couldn't get the handbills
out in time,' they would say. Or: 'It's the apathy, you know. Can't
get 'em out these days – they won't leave the television.'

Well, why the hell did you ask me to come? he always wanted
to say. But he never said it.

He wondered what the excuse would be at Earnley....

'You're Johnnie Byrne,' said the mayor, with a broad and
comfortable Yorkshire accent. It suited his chubby face, his black
homburg and double-breasted black overcoat. The mayor was a
man of substance. He moved and spoke with ponderous
assurance. 'I'm afraid there's not much of a crowd. The rain has
ruined it. Lovely crowd we had up till half past three.' He took
Byrne's elbow and hustled him along. 'Near on two thousand we
had. Then there was a cloudburst and they all traipsed off home.
Never mind, we got the entrance money. Probably make fifty
quid all told.'

Byrne clucked sympathetically and hunched his shoulders against the rain which had fallen since the train left Doncaster. He had shuddered as the first streaks whipped along the carriage windows. Hell of a day to address the Earnley Labour Party and Trades Council Joint Annual Whit Monday Fête and Gala. Well, here he was. He rigged a cheerful grin across his face.

'Such is life, brother,' he said, because he could think of nothing better to say.

'I've brought the official car along,' said the mayor diffidently, but with lurking pride. 'Couldn't dare do it but I'm attending in an official capacity, see. You and me judge the fancy dress, then I give the prizes and you make the speech.'

The mayor stood at the kerb-side and waved to a chauffeur.

'Come on, Albert lad,' he shouted, benevolent, fraternal and democratic in his deployment of the christian name. He bustled around the car with proprietary pride and settled Byrne in the back seat, tucking a rug over his knees....

The mayoral limousine swept through the gates of the football ground, through the crowds of wet parents taking their soaked children home to dry out in front of the fire. The amplifiers were beating out a Sousa march from a gramophone record, thumping it over the bruised grass and the mud, to the dripping sideshows to the silver-wet tents and low clouds. What was left of the crowd sheltered in the refreshment marquee....

The chauffeur unlocked a case and fastened the Earnley chain over the mayor's shoulders. 'Very fine chain,' said the mayor, as the rain splashed down from the brim of his homburg. 'Come on, it might rust if we get it wet.' He laughed hugely and thrust Byrne towards the shelter of the marquee. 'I don't really mean that,' he explained, 'silver gilt this chain is. It won't rust in a thousand years'.

They squelched through the mud. The marquee was heavy with the summer smell of dank trodden grass mixed with steam from the tea-urns and the whiff of wet raincoats. The gloom inside was as depressing as the rain outside. Byrne felt his misery rising to choke him, overwhelmed by the jostling closeness of damp and dismal people.

... This was the movement – the knockers-on-doors, the brewers-of-tea, the folk who laboured to keep politics alive, the people who were impassioned about the minutes of the Street

Lighting Committee and the H-bomb, who were all for disarmament and all against war. Then he felt a quirk of shame, not in repentance at his previous mood, but at the superior and sentimental tenor of his new mood. Who was he to patronize them? Perhaps they still saw a truth which he had forgotten. Perhaps their hearts had stayed alive while his had died. And, anyway, they were not so holy themselves. Some of the most diabolical elbow work and eye gouging in politics happened in the jungle of local politics.

In a moment he found himself, cup of tea in hand, listening to the mayor.

William Fienburgh, *No Love for Johnnie*, London, 1959, pp. 5–10.

1.17   A women's section in action

The main function of Labour women during this period was usually that of, in Fienburgh's words, 'brewers-of-tea'. By no means all women were unhappy with this limited role. Whilst women's sections usually discussed policy at one time or another, a good number were usually little more than afternoon gatherings of friends. This was certainly the case in Liverpool's West Toxteth ward.

The chairman said she was glad to see a few more members present although some were still off with colds, etc. The weather had been very severe but we hope we had the worst of it now.

Secretary presented the balance sheet for the year 1958. It had not been a good year either financially or with membership, we had lost two of our very old members – and we are unable to persuade younger people to join. After members accepted the balance sheet we had election of officers. These remaining en bloc as last year.

We had a draw won by Mrs Young – who gave it back for another draw. Tea.

Merseyside Records Office, 331 TLP/3, Toxteth Constituency Labour Party papers, West Toxteth women's section minute book, 1951–60: minute for 27 January 1959.

2

The Gaitskellite challenge, 1959–63

Labour's failure to win the 1959 election initiated a period of open conflict between the mainly Gaitskellite leadership and largely left-wing Party activists over public ownership and unilateral nuclear disarmament. Quick on the heels of defeat, Gaitskell tried to win support for a thorough remodelling of Labour. To this end, he announced his desire to revise clause iv, section 4 of the Party's constitution. Yet, on this specific issue Gaitskell was opposed by old allies in the unions as well as accustomed enemies in the constituencies. Moreover, this disagreement coincided with the rise of support for the Campaign for Nuclear Disarmament (CND) within Labour's ranks. Gaitskell opposed CND. Despite this, the 1960 Party conference voted in favour of unilateralism. Gaitskell refused to accept this decision and led a campaign against it. Unwilling to continue this damaging confrontation with the PLP, the 1961 conference acceded to the leader's wishes. The effect of this period of struggle was mixed. Whilst Gaitskell's authority within the Party had been temporarily enhanced, Labour's attitude to public ownership continued to be ambiguous whilst Party organisation remained unsatisfactory.

2.1 The need to change

In the weeks following the 1959 defeat, Gaitskell and his supporters made their case for fundamental change within the Party. There appeared to be something of a consensus within the PLP. This embraced Gaitskellites, avowed pragmatists such as James Callaghan and even the renegade Bevanite Richard Crossman. Tony Benn,[1] at this time standing in the Party's centre, recorded in his diary conversations with many of the leading figures.

[11 October 1959] To the Gaitskells'. Hugh was tired but mellow and said he wanted a holiday, which he deserved....

He also said several times, 'I'm not prepared to lose another Election for the sake of nationalisation.' He laid great stress on the disadvantages of the name Labour, particularly on new housing estates, and said, 'Of course Douglas Jay[2] is going to urge us to adopt a new one.' I reminded him that the prune had been resuscitated without a change of name by clever selling.

Hugh also thought we must review our relations with the trade unions especially the need for greater freedom and in local authorities.

Dora [Gaitskell] was bubbling with hate of left and right. She is game.

[12 October] Flew home from London and saw Roy Jenkins[3] on *Panorama* advocating very modestly that you should drop nationalisation, watch out for the dangers of the union links and not rule out an association with the Liberals.

He dropped in here on his way back home and we had a flaming row. As a matter of fact I was very calm and collected and he got into a semi-hysterical state. Usually it's the other way round. 'We must use this shock to drop nationalisation entirely at this forthcoming Conference,' he said, and I concentrated on the dangers to our integrity if we were to be so reckless. In the end he half apologised for his temper and went off with Jennifer [Jenkins].

[13 October] I rang Dick Crossman and told him that Roy was very definite against nationalisation. Dick said he thought we'd have to drop it, but not now. And I was a bit surprised to find myself on the left in this argument.

[15 October] Spoke to Jim Callaghan, who wants Bevan to be Deputy Leader and thinks we must rethink our nationalisation.

[1 November] To the London Labour Party Youth School. They all agree that trade unions, local councils and nationalisation had harmed us in the Election but none of them wanted to break with the past.

Tony Benn, *Years of Hope. Diaries, Papers and Letters 1940–1962*, edited by Ruth Winstone, London, 1994, pp. 317–19.

2.2 *Tribune*'s interpretation of defeat

In contrast to Gaitskell, *Tribune* viewed Labour's third successive defeat as proving that the Party had to return to 'socialism'. Thus, the leadership needed to emphasise planning and nationalisation rather than shy away from such policies. *Tribune* also saw merit in stressing the need for nuclear disarmament. In other words, Labour had to give society a moral lead.

The Tories have received a mandate to perpetuate the kind of society in which they believe – the unjust society, the casino society, the ugly society....

The unjust society now has the acquiescence of a larger number of voters, and a bigger majority in Parliament, than at any time since 1935. There can be no shying away either from the real meaning of this election result or from the shadow it casts over Britain's future.

During the post-war years, millions of our people have been subtly acclimatised to the acceptance of the unjust society, not only by potent methods of propaganda, but by a style of living and a concept of social relations geared to that society....

Well, how has it happened? Is there something inherently wrong with the British people, that they should turn aside from the just society and from the ideals they prized fourteen years ago?

That is not the answer. The truth is that they have been given no true alternative. Nobody has taught them to do otherwise than pant after the scramble for personal prizes, scream their applause and envy at the catchword 'double your money', and gape in awe at the inane rituals of royalty, of the titled and of the privileged....

At each election, Labour makes less and less of a challenge to the unjust society; gives the Tories more and more of their fundamental case; abandons another chunk of its ideals. And at each election Labour loses more seats. The amazing thing is that anyone should suggest that the solution is to complete the disastrous process, scrap what remains of distinctive Socialist ideas, and merge with the Liberals....

Labour will catch the ear of the nation only when it makes a forthright and credible challenge to the present social system.

Tribune, 16 October 1959.

2.3   Gaitskell's speech to conference

The 1959 Party conference was held within weeks of Labour's defeat. Gaitskell used his speech to delegates to call for the abolition of clause iv, section 4. This initiated one of the most fraught periods in Labour's history, bringing to a head a conflict which had been developing since the early 1950s.

2.3(a)   **Why Labour lost**

Gaitskell began by underlining the seriousness of Labour's deteriorating electoral position. He sought to identify the causes of this adverse trend.

It is, I believe, a significant change in the economic and social background of politics. First, there is the changing character of the labour force. There are fewer miners, more engineers; fewer farm workers, more shop assistants; fewer manual workers, more clerical workers; fewer railwaymen, more research workers. Everywhere the balance is shifting away from heavy, physical work and towards machine maintenance, distribution and staff jobs. Go to any large works in the country, as I happened to have done a good deal in the last couple of years, and you will find exactly the same story. It is an inevitable result of technological advance. But it means that the typical worker of the future is more likely to be a skilled man in a white overall, watching dials in a bright new modern factory than a badly paid cotton operative working in a dark and obsolete 19th-Century mill. The second great change is the absence of serious unemployment or even the fear of it.... In the inter-war years it was never less than 10 per cent. It permeated the lives of the British people. Serious slumps at more or less regular intervals were a normal part of our existence – and, incidentally, an important cause of the swing of the political pendulum. They were a constant reminder that a system which permitted such misery and waste was a failure; they were part of the practical basis of our Socialist propaganda.

Moreover, the recent improvements in living standards have been of a special kind. There has been a particularly notable increase in comforts, pleasures and conveniences in the home. Television, whether we like it or not, has transformed the leisure hours of the vast majority of our fellow-citizens. Washing machines, refrigerators, modern cookers, have made women's lives a good deal easier. And incidentally, I fancy that our failure this time was largely a failure to win support from the women.... It is no use dismissing the problem, as some do, by saying that women are too snobbish or too politically apathetic. They are voters and count just as much as men....

2.3(b)   The problem with public ownership

According to Gaitskell, the key to the Party's problems was its association with public ownership. Whilst seeing it as a potentially useful policy – in certain circumstances – Gaitskell wanted to distance Labour from it: nationalisation was, he suggested, merely a means and not an end in itself.

Now I turn to public ownership and nationalisation. There seems no doubt that, if we are to accept the majority view of those who fought this election, nationalisation – on balance – lost us votes....

Why was nationalisation apparently a vote loser? For two reasons I believe. First, some of the existing nationalised industries are unpopular. This unpopularity is very largely due to circumstances which have nothing to do with nationalisation.... The backward condition of the railways are not really the result of bad management but of inadequate investment in the past which has left behind a gigantic problem of modernisation....

The second reason ... was the confusion in the public mind about our future policy.... Our moderate, practical proposals were distorted out of all recognition by our opponents.... They were led to suppose we were going to take over everything indiscriminately, right and left, when we got back into power, simply out of a doctrinaire belief in public ownership. There was of course no relationship between these fears and the actual content of our programme.

... Some suggest that we should accept for all time the present frontiers between the public and private sectors. We cannot do that. It would imply that everything works so perfectly in the private sector that we shall never want to intervene. But things are far from perfect in the private sector.... I cannot agree that we have reached the frontier of public ownership as a whole.

At the same time I disagree equally with the other extreme view that nationalisation or even public ownership is the be all and end all, the ultimate first principle and aim of socialism. I believe that this view arises from a complete confusion about the fundamental meaning of socialism and, in particular, a misunderstanding about ends and means.

2.3(c) The need for a new Party constitution

To signify Labour's new attitude to the economy, Gaitskell wanted clause iv, section 4 revised.

As I have already said I am against starting on a new election programme now. But I do think that we should clear our minds on these fundamental issues and then try to express in the most simple and comprehensive fashion what we stand for in the world today.

The only official document which embodies such an attempt is the Party Constitution, written over 40 years ago. It seems to me that this needs to be brought up to date. For instance, can we really be satisfied today with a statement of fundamentals which makes no mention at all of colonial freedom, race relations, disarmament, full employment or planning? The only specific reference to our objectives at home is the well-known phrase:

'To secure for the workers by hand or brain the full fruits of their industry and the most equitable distribution thereof that may be possible, upon the basis of the common ownership of the means of production, distribution and exchange....'

Standing on its own, this cannot possibly be regarded as adequate. It lays us open to continual misrepresentation. It implies that common ownership is an end, whereas in fact it is a means. It implies that the only precise object we have is nationalisation, whereas in fact we have many other Socialist objectives. It implies that we propose to nationalise everything, but do we? ... Of course not. We have long ago come to accept, we know very well, for the foreseeable future, at least in some form, a mixed economy; in which case, if this is our view – as I believe it to be of 90 per cent of the Labour Party – had we not better say so instead of going out of our way to court misrepresentation? ...

I am sure that the Webbs and Arthur Henderson who largely drafted this Constitution, would have been amazed and horrified had they thought that their words were to be treated as sacrosanct 40 years later in utterly changed conditions. Let us remember that we are a Party of the future, not of the past; that we must appeal to the young as well as the old – young people who have very little reverence for the past. It is no use waving banners of a bygone age.

Report of the Fifty-Eighth Annual Conference of the Labour Party, London, 1959, pp. 107–9.

2.4 One member's opinion

> The problem with revising clause iv was that it possessed a symbolic importance to many in both the Party and unions. The strength of this attachment was made clear in a letter sent to Labour's general secretary from a Scottish stalwart.

Dear Sir and Comrade,

in the first instance let me state that I could write page upon page on the topic I am about to write on but considering all circumstances I will have to content myself with a brief letter.

I have been a member of my Individual Section of the Labour Party for 32 years, an affiliated member of my trade-union for 35 years and before that a member of the ILP [Independent Labour Party] Guild of Youth for 5 years. I assume you have no need to question my loyalty; moreover I have held all kinds of official positions in the Movement between my political party and my

Trade-union, been active all my working life in all phases of activity national and local, on three occasions I have turned down invitations to stand as a candidate for parliamentary honours but aware of my shortcomings I declined. However to talk about myself is not the purpose of this letter. The topic mentioned above is Clause 4 of the Constitution of the Labour Party hence the second letter to you during my life-time.

When in my 'teens I grappled mentally with all the questions afflicting our family poverty (I was one of 8) and in order to find the answers I decided to join the Movement expecting to change the order of things that brought about so much social injustice. I fought and lived in hope that the theory of 'the inevitability of gradualness'[4] would prevail. I still cherish that hope and I expect you will understand what goes on in my mind as a consequence however after a life-time of the hard core of experience and now confronted with the silver spoon theories of 'dons' concerning *clause 4* [*sic*]. I hereby accord my protest to any action to alter the *constitution* of the Party to which I am proud to belong. Thank you for your indulgence.

LPA, Morgan Phillips's papers, GS/CMR/102, letter from David McCreath to Morgan Phillips, dated 12 March 1960.

2.5 Labour's new values

> Owing to lack of support on the NEC, Gaitskell was unable to replace Labour's formal commitment to nationalisation. Instead, he was allowed to add a further statement of aims to clause iv. This was widely described by Party members as the 'New Testament' and contained twelve sections, the ones pertaining to domestic policy being included below.

The British Labour Party is a democratic socialist party. Its central ideal is the brotherhood of man. Its purpose is to make this ideal a reality elsewhere.

Accordingly:

a) It rejects discrimination on grounds of race, colour or creed and holds that men should accord to one another equal consideration and status in recognition of the fundamental dignity of man....

e) It stands for social justice, for a society in which the claims of those in hardship or distress come first; where the wealth produced by all is fairly shared among all; where differences in rewards depend not upon birth or inheritance but on the effort, skill and creative energy contributed to the common good; and where equal opportunities exist for all to live a full and varied life.

f) Regarding the pursuit of material wealth by and for itself as empty and barren, it rejects the selfish, acquisitive doctrines of capitalism, and strives to create instead a socialist community based on fellowship, co-operation and service in which all can share fully in our cultural heritage.

g) Its aim is a classless society from which all class barriers and false social values have been eliminated.

h) It holds that to ensure full employment, rising production, stable prices and steadily advancing living standards the nation's economy should be planned and all concentrations of power subordinated to the interests of the community as a whole.

i) It stands for democracy in industry, and for the right of the workers both in the public and private sectors to full consultation in all the vital decisions of management, especially those affecting conditions of work.

j) It is convinced that these social and economic objectives can be achieved only through an expansion of common ownership substantial enough to give the community power over the commanding heights of the economy. Common ownership takes varying forms, including state-owned industries and firms, producer and consumer co-operation, municipal ownership and public participation in private concerns. Recognising that both public and private enterprise have a place in the economy it believes that further extension of common ownership should be decided from time to time in the light of these objectives and according to circumstances, with due regard to the views of the workers and consumers concerned.

k) It stands for the happiness and freedom of the individual against the glorification of the state – for the protection of workers, consumers and all citizens against any exercise of arbitrary power, whether by the state, by private or by public authorities, and it will resist all forms of collective prejudice and intolerance.

Report of the Fifty-Ninth Annual Conference of the Labour Party, London, 1960, p. 12.

2.6   Gaitskell spoiling for a fight

Frustrated in his ambition to transform the Party's ideological character through clause iv, Gaitskell looked on the growing support for unilateralism as an alternative way of achieving his aim. Thus, he deliberately provoked a fight with the left by rejecting the caution of some of his advisers. One of these was Patrick Gordon Walker,[5] whose diary gives an insight into the leader's combative mood.

I had my first serious disagreement with Gaitskell. This was in a very long discussion at Roy Jenkins' flat with Tony Crosland and G[aitskell]. We met after the House rose, from about 10.30 to 1 a.m.

I began to fear that G has the seeds of self destruction in him – he almost wants to destroy himself. I said at one point that he had a death wish. He is becoming distrustful and angry with his best friends and wants to take up absolute and categorical positions that will alienate all but a handful.

Subject of discussion was the upsurge of pacifism in the Trade Unions. G said it was certain that a pacifist resolution would be carried at Conference. The alternatives would then be: (a) to carry the Parly [Parliamentary] party into defiance of the Conference; (b) to go into opposition in the party on this issue – with perhaps 100 supporters – and fight back from the back benches. 'It would be a relief to be able to talk frankly and without compromise.'...

We spent much time on the principles on which we would stand. I said of course we must stand on principle. I suggested: acceptance of responsibility for national defence – collective security – NATO, 'in which there must be a nuclear deterrent'.... If a pacifist resolution was passed we must say we disagreed with it and stand for the Parly Cttee. It would not be a question of a dramatic defiance of Conference but of a long fight to get things right again, holding on to all the positions of authority we could. No-one could survive who set himself against the whole fabric and structure of the party.

G wanted to go much further. He wanted to say specifically that we should retain and use nuclear weapons as loyal members of the NATO alliance. I said this was madness. This was the sort of thing a professor or journalist could say, but not a political leader.

Robert Pearce (ed.), *Patrick Gordon Walker. Political Diaries, 1932–1971*, London, 1991: entry for 12 May 1960, p. 259.

2.7   Gaitskell's speech to the 1960 conference

Having rejected conciliation, Gaitskell gave a defiant speech before conference voted on unilateralism. Whereas some commentators viewed his performance in heroic terms, others in the Party, in this instance the former Bevanite Barbara Castle,[6] were less impressed. Indeed, she suggests in her autobiography that Gaitskell made his defeat all the more likely by being so uncompromising. That, so far as Gaitskell was concerned, was the point. By this stage, he saw defeat as serving a wider purpose.

Gaitskell ... opened by listing all the points on which we were agreed, but the medieval-schoolman streak in him got the better of him and he launched into a remarkable attack on Cousins,[7] accusing him of guilt by inference. Some people might say, he argued, that the meaning of his resolution was not clear, but it was clear to him. Whatever the words said, it was inspired by those who wanted to lead us into unilateralism and neutralism. To cap it all, Gaitskell threw down the gauntlet of defiance to conference, warning that Labour MPs would never accept the Cousins resolution whatever the conference said. He ended with a dramatic peroration: 'There are some of us, Mr Chairman, who will fight and fight and fight again to save the party we love.' I have seldom heard a more effectively counter-productive speech. At one stroke Gaitskell had damaged two of the causes he held dear. In the first place, conference proceeded to adopt the Cousins resolution and reject the NEC statement, though by a narrow majority, and even narrowly carried the Amalgamated Engineering Union resolution, the only one to demand Britain's unilateral renunciation of nuclear weapons. In the second place, he widened the breach between conference and the parliamentary party and intensified the determination of the rank and file to break the MPs' monopoly of the election of the leadership.

Barbara Castle, *Fighting all the Way*, London, 1993, p. 325.

2.8   The Campaign for Democratic Socialism

After his defeat, Gaitskell's supporters attempted to reverse support for unilateralism in CLPs and trade unions. Leading this fight was the Campaign for Democratic Socialism (CDS). As the name implies, members of CDS did not see the leadership's reverse on nuclear weapons in isolation, but – like Gaitskell – viewed it as part of a wider ideological battle against the left.

This [conference support for unilateralism] is the culmination of a long period in which the voice of moderate opinion in the Labour Party has been drowned by the clamour of an active and articulate minority. As Socialists who are loyal to its central tradition yet aware of the changed conditions of the nineteen-sixties, we seek to reassert the views of the great mass of Labour supporters against those of doctrinaire pressure-groups.

By the central tradition of the Party we mean a non-doctrinal, practical, humanitarian socialism – a creed of conscience and reform rather than of class hatred. The British Labour Movement owes its inspiration to British radicals, trade unionists, co-operators, nonconformists and christian socialists, not to Marx or Lenin....

We believe that the Labour party should be a broadly-based national party of all the people, as the early pioneers saw it. To their vision we wish to return. A democratic socialist party must be based predominantly on working people. But a purely sectional, one-class party would face electoral suicide; more importantly, it would be a betrayal of the ideal of a classless society....

We interpret socialism not as an arid economic dogma, but in terms of freedom, equality, social justice and world co-operation. We believe that the British people, who rightly mistrust doctrinaire utopianism, will always respond to an idealistic appeal to remedy real evils by practical and radical reform.

BLPES, Anthony Crosland papers, 6/1, manifesto of the Campaign for Democratic Socialism, issued October 1960.

2.9   The need to attract housewives

As Gaitskell's 1959 speech (document 2.3) had made clear, he was most concerned to win the support of young married women, many of whom voted Conservative. This report, intended for discussion at a meeting of leading Labour women in Yorkshire, gives an insight into their view of the housewife 'problem'. It would inform the national Party's subsequent propaganda.

One conclusion widely reached in our examination of the General Election is that we failed to attract support from women electors – particularly young married women in the 25 to 45 age group. This is perhaps not surprising in view of the fact that the Election was fought in an atmosphere of 'Conservative Prosperity' which Labour was successfully depicted as being out to 'ruin'. The impact of prosperity (and of poverty) is nowhere more deeply felt than in the home, and home to the housewife, irrespective of whether she goes out to work or merely remains at home, is the focal point of her life. Consequently, she is very susceptible to propaganda of the type to which we were subjected in the period leading up to and in the General Election itself....

How can we win over the votes of women electors?

The first essential is to appreciate that future elections will no doubt be fought in a similar atmosphere of relative prosperity. This means that appeals to vote Labour in order to prevent a return to pre-war conditions of slumps and unemployment will cut little ice with the young housewife today. Her life is one in which a new house (Council or private), a family car, a television, an electric washer, cooker, and perhaps even a 'frig', predominate.

If she does not already possess all these things then she aspires to do so as quickly as possible, and the 'telly' is a daily reminder that life is not complete without them.

Halifax Public Library, Calderdale Archives, Halifax Constituency Labour Party papers, TU 28/16, miscellaneous correspondence, 1959–60, Yorkshire Regional Office of the Labour Party, 'Report on Women's Organisation for consideration at special meetings of Women's Advisory Councils with the Chief Woman Officer on 13th, 14th and 15th January, 1960', January 1960.

2.10   Strain in the ranks

In the midst of the conflict over clause iv and unilateralism, ordinary Party members tried to keep their organisations running and even improve them – as exhorted by Gaitskell. Yet, too few put in the necessary effort. The minutes of one local party in the industrial north-west of England reveal how it could become too much for the minority of activists.

Matters arising. Secretary's resignation. Mrs Nadin was asked to reconsider her decision to resign from the position of Secretary. She stated that although she enjoyed doing the work she did not see why she should be the butt of the recent criticism which had been levelled at her. There was a complete lack of liaison between the Local Party and the Constituency Office, and this did not make the job any easier when you had to deal with people who were not prepared to co-operate. The G.C. [General Committee] had not done their duty as a Committee, when any major decision had to be made it was always moved that the Secretary and Chairman deal with the matter, or the matter be left to the Officers and this threw more than the fair share of the running of the Party on to too few people. Attendances at both the G.C. and E.C. [Executive Committee] had been very discouraging, and the Secretary pointed out that she herself had not missed a meeting for three years, this included quite a few Sunday morning meetings during the time of elections. Mrs Sidebottom then stated that one should not go down after the first knock, but should rise smiling time after time. This might sound very bold and brave but the Secretary said that when she was trying to do a job that no one else was prepared to take on it was not her place to take the knocks as it were, but to have the help of every member of the G.C. and the E.C. behind her. The work would have to be shared out more over the Committee and not left to the Officers.

Tameside Local Studies, Ashton-under-Lyne Local Labour Party papers, DD88/3/2, Executive Committee minutes: minute for 27 January 1960.

2.11   Gateshead and the space age

> Housewives were but one of the groups Labour hoped to attract as voters and members. Some CLPs tried to make themselves more appealing by emphasising their social activities. In Gateshead, located in the Labour heartland of north-east England, such an initiative was apparently successful. Here is an admittedly rosy account of the enterprise.

A Labour space-age club for 3–13 year olds that bulges at the seams – a Labour old people's club that sits down 200 at its annual dinner. Those are at the two ends of Gateshead's 'Cradle to the Grave' programme. And these are not proposals, they are live flourishing enterprises.

To keep pace with its 'new look' the Gateshead Labour Party has provided the Young Socialists with their own coffee-bar and independent meeting room. These were provided by the conversion of two very dilapidated attic rooms by part voluntary and part time paid labour in which the Young Socialists themselves played an active part. The coffee-bar is decorated in a modern contemporary colour scheme chosen by themselves and has modern furnishings which although still not complete, help to create the atmosphere necessary to attract the youth of our modern atomic age....

Last September we decided that it is not enough for the Labour Party to boast loudly of its regard for old folk and their problems and indeed, is the only political party that really means what it says. We decided that we were still not meeting local needs and still not setting the necessary example, so we launched a Gateshead Labour Hall Old Folks and Supporters Club.... The supporters in the club help to make the old folk comfortable by preparing and serving the refreshments, sending them birthday cards and visiting them when they are sick. Just before Christmas over 200 sat down in the Town Hall for the Club's First Annual Dinner, at which the guest speaker was the M.P. for Gateshead West, Mr. Harry Randall. Discussions are now taking place in the Club committee (freely and democratically elected by the old folk) with a view to affiliating to the party and sending delegates to the G.M.C.

Having dealt with the needs of youth and the old folk and knowing, as indeed all Parties do, that the women's sections are very capable of looking after themselves, we set about catering for the children of school-age but too young for the Young Socialists. We decided to make it known as the Gateshead Labour Hall Space-Age Club and to invite membership from among Party members. After only a few weeks and with Christmas intervening, we have a membership of just over 50, which is as much as the four voluntary women section helpers can manage with, for their ages range from 3–13 years....

These children and the old folk get used to coming to Labour Hall each week and look to us for help. One good turn deserves another and ultimately it will reflect itself in good Labour votes.

Labour Organiser, 40:464, February 1961, pp. 25–6.

2.12 Gateshead and 'tripe'

Initiatives such as Gateshead's did not generate universal approval. This letter from an anonymous Party agent revealed that the belief that Labour should remain a working-class and purely 'political' organisation would take a long time to die.

What a load of gimmick-dressed tripe we've been getting in the *Organiser* recently. An agent boasts about acting as nursemaid to a group of toddlers he calls a space age club. He also helps grandma's with their knitting. Other agents set up coffee bars for teenagers who proceed in many cases to wreck the joints.

Women organisers run luncheon clubs and dinner parties, and Sheffield has even given up May-day, the day of traditional working-class solidarity and replaced it by a time of petty bourgeois wine bibbing. No doubt guests will rise to their feet and sing (after a famous columnist):

'The people's flag has gone you see,
'Twas stolen by the bourgeoisie'....

I suppose I am a dyed in the wool old-timer, but what the hell are we coming to? Where is the real hard core of our organisation? And where will all these up-to-date silly gimmicks lead us?·

Labour Organiser, 40:465, March 1961, p. 54.

2.13   The death of Gaitskell

After a brief illness Gaitskell died in January 1963. His loyal band of followers, many of whom occupied senior positions in the PLP, were naturally distraught. Gaitskell, they felt, had been cheated of becoming Prime Minister, a post he would have occupied with unique distinction. They would later compare the shortcomings of Harold Wilson, Gaitskell's successor, with the idealised attributes of Labour's lost leader. In his autobiography, Douglas Jay spoke for many Gait- skellites.

Gaitskell's death at this moment was, I believed that night, and am even more certain in the retrospect of over fifteen years, not merely an inexpressible tragedy for his friends and the Labour Movement, but a catastrophe for the nation. For he not merely possessed the pre-eminent straightforwardness, common sense and moral authority of Attlee, but a wider intelligence and a deeper understanding of the economic and social issues of the age than any of his contemporaries in British politics.... If he had lived, the future of this country would ... have been far different and far happier.... [H]e would, as the public were beginning to realize in the last year of his life, have exercised, like Attlee and Cripps, a moral influence over his Party and British politics generally in the 1960s and 1970s, which was sorely needed and sadly lacking....

I was driven back that evening of 18 January 1963, from Sunderland to Newcastle, realizing all too well that the whole future had become grim and unpredictable. Indeed I wondered whether it was any good staying in politics at all. For want of advice and comfort from somebody, I later asked Herbert Bowden, Labour Chief Whip, a colleague respected by all of us, and a most loyal friend and admirer of Gaitskell, what he meant to do. 'I shall carry on,' Bowden said, 'so far as is humanly possible.'

Douglas Jay, *Change and Fortune*, London, 1980, pp. 287–8.

3

The natural party of government, 1963–70

Harold Wilson succeeded Hugh Gaitskell in February 1963. As leader, Wilson was in a difficult position: probably all the shadow cabinet voted against him whilst many backbench MPs supported his candidacy only because they considered his nearest rival, George Brown,[1] too uncertain a prospect. Such doubts were temporarily put to one side, however, as the Party faced an imminent election. Wilson's 'white heat' rhetoric seemed to win favour with voters outside the manual working class and appeared likely to give Labour the edge over the Conservatives. In the event, Labour achieved only a slim majority in 1964; this was substantially increased by the 1966 general election. Yet, this latter triumph was not the precursor to great legislative achievements. The government's response to Britain's severe economic problems strained its relationship with the trade unions; caused demoralisation in the Party's ranks; and led to a dramatic loss of electoral support. Despite Wilson's description of Labour as the 'natural party of government', by 1968 it looked set to be swept away into electoral oblivion.

3.1 Wilson and the Gaitskellites

Gaitskell's shadow cabinet was mainly composed of loyal supporters. They detested Wilson for being a Bevanite and standing against the leader in 1960. Thus, as Richard Crossman's diary makes clear, Wilson considered himself at odds with most colleagues. This isolated position would feed Wilson's later belief that members of the cabinet constantly plotted his removal.

[15 February 1963] I took an hour and a half off with Roy and Jennifer Jenkins to lunch at the Athenaeum. I particularly wanted to find out what they were thinking. Both of them were completely knocked out by Gaitskell's death ... I felt them to be generally in mourning for Gaitskell and not particularly enthusiastic for Brown.... Nevertheless Roy was as implacable as ever and I spent most of lunch trying to make him say what makes him support a thug like Brown against a man of Wilson's quality. Jenkins found it surprisingly difficult. First he tried to call Harold intellectually dishonest but he really couldn't pretend that Douglas Jay or Patrick Gordon Walker show greater intellectual integrity. All Roy could say was that it was worse in Harold's case because he was more gifted.

Roy also indignantly denied the charge of jealousy, though I don't think he quite convinced himself on that score. I said, 'But wasn't it a hallmark of a Gaitskellite to be anti-Wilson? Wasn't a condition of your group, to jump on Harold ever since Hugh Dalton called him Nye's [Bevan's] little dog? And wasn't Hugh the cause of the trouble?' Roy at once denied this about Hugh. 'Indeed,' he said, 'at one of his last talks with me, he said that at least Harold was predictable, whereas Callaghan was completely unpredictable, in seeking his personal self-interest.' Finally Roy said, 'The fact is that Harold is a person no one can like, a person without friends.'

[12 March] We had a most interesting evening last Sunday when Barbara Castle invited Harold Wilson to supper to meet Judith Hart,[2] Michael Foot, George Wigg,[3] Tony Greenwood[4] and myself. It was an interesting test of how Harold would behave to his old friends of the Left. He could not have been nicer, more natural or more shrewd. He was relaxed, completely frank and easy and yet careful not to promise more than he could fulfil. 'You must understand that I am running a Bolshevik Revolution with a Tsarist Shadow Cabinet,' he remarked, and explained how bitterly hostile and suspicious most of these miserable creatures are.

Janet Morgan (ed.), *The Backbench Diaries of Richard Crossman*, London, 1981, pp. 979–80, 987.

3.2 White heat

At the Party's 1963 conference, Wilson asserted that only Labour could ensure Britain's prosperity in the midst of the 'white heat' of technological change. He argued that Labour's state planning and intervention – not necessarily nationalisation – would help the economy to adapt. In so doing, he hoped to convince middle-class and 'affluent' working-class voters that Labour would increase their personal wealth. His call for 'new attitudes' from both sides of industry also suggested that trade unions would find Wilson critical of some of their practices.

The Britain that is going to be forged in the white heat of this revolution will be no place for restrictive practices or for outdated methods on either side of industry. We shall need a totally new attitude to the problems of apprenticeship, of training and re-training for skill. If there is one thing where the traditional philosophy of capitalism breaks down it is in training for apprenticeship, because quite frankly it does not pay any individual firm, unless it is very altruistic or quixotic or farsighted, to train apprentices if it knows at the end of the period of training they will be snapped up by some unscrupulous firm that makes no contribution to apprenticeship training. That is what economists mean when they talk about the difference between marginal private cost and net social cost.

So we are going to need a new attitude. In some industries we shall have to get right away from the idea of apprenticeship to a single firm. There will have to be apprenticeship with the industry as a whole, and the industry will have to be responsible for it. Indeed, if we are going to end demarcation and snobbery in our training for skill and for science why should not these apprenticeship contracts be signed with the State itself? Then again, in the Cabinet room and the board room alike those charged with the control of our affairs must be ready to think and to speak in the language of our scientific age.

For the commanding heights of British industry to be controlled today by men whose only claim is their aristocratic connections or the power of inherited wealth or speculative finance is as irrelevant to the twentieth century as would be the continued purchase of commissions in the armed forces by lordly amateurs. At the very time that even the MCC[5] has abolished the distinction between amateurs and professionals, in science and industry we are content to remain a nation of Gentleman in a world of Players.

For those who have studied the formidable Soviet challenge in the education of scientists and technologists, and above all, in the ruthless application of scientific techniques in Soviet industry, know that our future lies not in military strength alone but in the efforts, sacrifices, and above all the energies which a free people can mobilise for the future greatness of our country. Because we are democrats, we reject the methods which communist countries are deploying in applying the results of scientific research to industrial life. But because we care deeply about the future of Britain, we must use all the resources of democratic planning, all the latent and underdeveloped energies and skills of our people, to ensure Britain's standing in the world. That is the message which I believe will go out from this conference to the people of Britain and the people of the world.

Harold Wilson, *Purpose in Politics*, London, 1964, pp. 27–8.

3.3   The purpose of a Labour government

Wilson sought to extend Labour's appeal beyond the trade union movement. As this extract from a local Labour paper distributed in industrial west Yorkshire indicates, such a view was contested. Some in the Party were convinced that Labour's main purpose was simply to represent the interests of the organised working class. This difference of emphasis would become pronounced during Labour's period in office.

What is a Labour government for? The question needs to be asked for some of our leaders seem to have forgotten the answer!

A Labour government is to increase working-class living standards, to reduce the present gross inequalities between capital and labour and to increase working-class control over the economy by means of further nationalisation.

A chorus of voices echoing from the heights of the T.U.C. and the Labour Party leadership seem to have the order of priorities reversed. Already talk of go slow on wages, of long-term wage agreements, of wage restraint and statesmanlike responsibility are in the air.

All this may be very well for union leaders in the line for knighthoods, peerages, seats on the B.B.C., on nationalised boards, or any of the manifold well-paying patronages at the disposal of the Parliamentary majority. To the man on the shop floor it doesn't count one brass copper.

The unions created the Labour Party because they learnt by hard experience that what the wage bargain could take with one hand, the government could steal back with the other. The Labour Party exists for the unions, who pay for and finance it, and not as an easy ride to power for middle-class politicians at the trade unionists' expense.

The test of a Labour government will be what it does for the workers. Let's hear less talk of wage restraint and more promises of wage benefit. The time has come for us to hear more of what Labour is going to do for the unions, and less about what the unions are expected to sacrifice for Labour.

LPA, Local Party Papers Collection, *Huddersfield Citizen*, April 1964.

3.4   The promise of a 'New Britain'

One of the criticisms of Wilson's 1964–70 governments was that they promised far more than they delivered. This led to disillusion amongst those who had idealistically supported the Party. It is certainly true that Labour's 1964 manifesto made great claims for the future. All manifestos, however, could be found guilty on this count. It is, nevertheless, in retrospect, a remarkably optimistic document.

The world wants it and would welcome it. The British people *want* it, *deserve* it, and urgently *need* it.

And now, at last, the general election presents us with the exciting prospect of achieving it.

The dying months of a frustrating 1964 can be transformed into the launching pad for the New Britain of the late 1960's and early 1970's.

A New Britain –

>   *mobilising* the resources of technology under a national plan;

72

harnessing our national wealth in brains, our genius for scientific invention and medical discovery;
reversing the decline of thirteen wasted years;
affording a new opportunity to equal, and if possible surpass, the roaring progress of other western powers while Tory Britain has moved sideways, backwards but seldom forwards.

The country needs fresh and virile leadership.

Labour is ready. Poised to swing its plans into instant operation. Impatient to apply the New Thinking that will end the chaos and sterility.

... We do not delude ourselves that the tasks ahead will be easy to accomplish. Even now we do not know the full extent of the damage we shall have to repair after thirteen wasted years of Conservative government. The essential conditions for success are, however, clear.

... we must foster, throughout the nation, a new and more critical spirit. In the place of the cosy complacency of the past thirteen years, we shall seek to evoke an active and searching frame of mind in which all of us, individuals, enterprises and trade unions are ready to re-examine our methods of work, to innovate and to modernise.

... we must put an end to the dreary commercialism and personal selfishness which have dominated the years of Conservative government. The morality of money and property is a dead and deadening morality. In its place we must again reassert the value of service above private profit and private gain.

The Labour Party is offering Britain a new way of life that will stir our hearts, re-kindle an authentic patriotic faith in our future, and enable our country to re-establish itself as a stable force in the world today for progress, peace and justice.

It is within the personal power of every man and woman with a vote to guarantee that the British again become

THE GO-AHEAD PEOPLE WITH A SENSE OF NATIONAL PURPOSE, THRIVING IN AN EXPANDING COMMUNITY WHERE SOCIAL JUSTICE IS SEEN TO PREVAIL.

Labour Party, *Let's Go with Labour for the New Britain. The*

Labour Party's Manifesto for the 1964 General Election, London, 1964, pp. 3, 23–4.

3.5 The failed revolution

The intended motor of Labour's New Britain was economic expansion. The spark for this was to be supplied by the Department of Economic Affairs (DEA), led by George Brown, Wilson's idiosyncratic deputy. In his autobiography, an obviously disenchanted Brown considered that the DEA's failure was due to the lack of zeal of certain colleagues, principally, of course, Wilson.

The story of the D.E.A. ... is the record of a social revolution that failed. The D.E.A. was meant to be – and it might have been – the greatest contribution of the Labour Party to the recasting of the machinery of government to meet the needs of the twentieth century. Its setting up was also the opening campaign of a major social revolution; its consequence – had it succeeded – more far reaching than anything else attempted by Labour since 1945. It envisaged a wholly novel form of national social accountancy to replace the orthodox financial accountancy by which the Treasury has always dominated British life.

The revolution failed – partly because it was betrayed by some of those who were pledged to see it through, and partly because ... fundamental changes in other policies were not carried out....

In 1963 I was chairman of the Home Policy Committee of the Labour Party, and we began to concert our planning for the General Election that would have come in 1964. At Transport House[6] we were already thinking of all kinds of ways of re-styling the Government.

Economic thinking was very much a part of this, and at that stage there was a considerable body of opinion which held that economic policy in Britain was too much subordinated to the financial considerations of the Treasury. We were all (at least, most of us who were concerned with Labour party policy) expansionists at heart, and we thought that the economy was being held back, that unemployment was being kept high, that all sorts of barriers were being erected to keep down industrial activity, by reason of the orthodox financial policy of the

Treasury. Out of this kind of thinking grew the idea that it would be better to have an economic department, which (as I always saw it) would be superior to the Treasury in determining the country's economic priorities.

Looking back, it seems that my own thinking may have gone farther ahead than that of the Prime Minister and some of my other colleagues, and it is possible that I made assumptions in my mind which the others did not, in fact, share.

George Brown, *In My Way*, Harmondsworth, 1972, pp. 87–9.

3.6 A fateful decision

One of the prime causes of the DEA's failure was the decision not to devalue sterling. Wilson, Brown and James Callaghan, the Chancellor of the Exchequer, were responsible for this fateful policy. Devaluation, some considered, would have made exports cheaper, thereby increasing the competitiveness of British goods and giving an important boost to the economy. Eventually the government was forced to devalue in November 1967: in the attempt to defend sterling it had lost millions from the financial reserve along with much political credibility. In his memoirs Callaghan defended the original 1964 decision: according to his account, the government had little choice in the matter.

Sterling's value has seesawed so dramatically in recent years that it is difficult to recreate at this distance of time how violently public and international sentiment opposed any idea of devaluing the second most important reserve currency in the world. It was almost a moral issue. One or two of my Oxford and Cambridge advisers, notably Professor Kaldor and Robert Neild, were in favour of an incoming Labour Government devaluing as soon as we took office, and they never swerved from that view. But theirs was a minority view which I resisted both for political and economic reasons. The Conservatives would have crucified us. It had taken several years for Labour to live down the taunts directed at us following the Cripps's devaluation in 1949, and if we had devalued on coming to power in October 1964 the Tory Opposition as well as the press would have hammered home day after day that devaluation was always Labour's soft option, and took place whenever a Labour Government was elected....

I was reinforced in my view when the result of the election became known and we emerged with a tiny working majority. If a devaluation is to be successful it must result in a reduction in the standard of living of the people. Given our minute majority, I did not see how we could hope to win the second general election that was bound to follow within a short time, with a sterling devaluation hanging around the Government's neck....

There were other important arguments. We should be embarking on a course the consequences of which I could not see. As all other nations at that time were opposed to a sterling devaluation, there was a danger that unilateral action by Britain might lead them to follow suit and protect themselves by devaluing their own currencies. In the process, they would deprive Britain of the competitive advantage we might otherwise gain.

... Then again, devaluation in 1964 would certainly hit those Commonwealth countries hardest who had voluntarily maintained their reserves in London, for it would have reduced their value in other currencies. And, finally, I feared that a devaluation that took the pressure temporarily off the pound would be regarded by my Cabinet colleagues as an opportunity to increase spending on all the schemes for social improvement with which we had come to office. Whereas, in truth, if it is to be successful, devaluation demanded the opposite.

James Callaghan, *Time and Chance*, London, 1987, pp. 159–60.

3.7   In power at last

After October 1964 Labour struggled on, despite its precarious position in the Commons. In March 1966 Wilson held another election, calculating correctly that this would give him a much more comfortable majority. Marcia Williams, his personal and political secretary, recalled the emotions of those in the Prime Minister's Downing Street 'kitchen cabinet' immediately after the results had been announced.

We had arrived at last. We had the measure of it all now; so we thought. We had fought to establish ourselves and had succeeded. We knew the ropes and we felt at last we could relax a little and try to enjoy 'being in power', whatever that might really mean.

The main thing about the 1964 election and the months that followed is that while many people in the Party may have felt power as such, I don't think that within No. 10 there was a feeling that the Government really possessed it. Over those first months there was a feeling of being squatters. The 1966 election was when the Government really got the first feeling of control and power. Now this particular feeling gave the inner confidence which had been so greatly needed and sadly lacking in 1964.

Now there were bouquets and gifts to welcome us back; congratulations and smiling faces on all sides. It was a most peculiar feeling suddenly to realise what it all meant; this was No. 10, Labour was in power, the power which the Labour Party had wanted for so long.

We were utterly tired and exhausted on that first morning, as one always is after an election. What I remember most of all despite the weariness was climbing into the lift with Harold to go up to the second floor; in answer to a query he looked at me most solemnly, saying in a very tired voice: 'Now we can have a rest from politics.' How wrong he was.

Marcia Williams, *Inside Number Ten*, London, 1975, p. 85

3.8 Interpreting Labour's 1966 victory

Labour's 1966 triumph was, in terms of Commons seats, impressive. It also saw the first rise in the Party's popular support since 1951. Yet, this turned out to be only a brief interlude in the Party's decline. In the face of contemporary optimism that Labour had become the 'natural party of government', this Party analysis of the election indicated that victory was less soundly based than some supposed.

Perhaps the most significant feature of the national statistics is the overall drop in *turn-out*, from 77.1% in 1964 to 75.8% on this occasion.... The continued decline in the overall percentage of people who actually go to the polls is not encouraging.

Although the result was undoubtedly good for the Labour Party, the gradual decline in the level of political interest, represented by the fall in the poll, hardly gives grounds for satisfaction. The Conservative vote has fallen by over 2 million since 1959, whilst Labour's has increased by something over 800,000, so although it is clear that the Conservatives have lost all the ground they gained in the 1950's, there has not been a corresponding increase in the degree of Labour support, even after 18 months of a Labour Government....

LPA, Home Policy Sub-Committee minutes, 11 July 1966, 'The 1966 General Election', Re/July 1966, p. 2.

3.9   The 'July measures'

> The government's real problems started soon after it had been re-elected. A sailor's strike undermined confidence in the economy, which led speculators to sell sterling. This forced the government to spend vital revenue to maintain sterling's value. By July 1966 this position had become unsustainable: the government either had to devalue or introduce deflationary measures to reassure speculators. Wilson was committed to avoiding devaluation, so deflation – which meant cuts in spending on social programmes, tax increases and limits on wages – was the favoured option. As Tony Benn's diary reveals, not all cabinet members favoured this option, whilst trade union leaders were overtly hostile.

[17 July 1966] At this moment, my thoughts are roughly this. I shall fight against the sort of Treasury cuts which would be socially inequitable and damaging to the growth of the economy. This is really a political crisis and when we have to choose what to cut it will be a test of our own political faith. The economists can't help us at this stage, beyond giving us a general indication of the lines on which we should go.

   [18 July] I decided to float around [the Commons] and talk to a few Ministers. I saw Fred Lee[7] whose main concern was that there should be appreciable defence cuts. I went to see George Brown and found him in a state of high excitement. Barbara

Castle was with him. He repeated definitely that he was going. He said that he had warned Harold a year ago that he was not prepared to put up with another episode of this kind and that Roy [Jenkins] and Tony [Crosland] agreed with him. Barbara said she thought there would be a majority in the Cabinet in favour of his view but George said that it was impossible that this could carry the day as Harold was so heavily committed publicly to maintaining the value of the pound. Barbara said she thought Harold would accept the majority view and George said, 'No, this involves the leadership. Do you want me as Leader, Barbara?' Barbara replied firmly, 'No.' 'Then Harold will win,' said George.

[19 July] At 2.30 the package of cuts arrived and I studied it briefly.

From 5 till 8.30 the Cabinet met. The big question was devaluation versus deflation. I spoke for devaluation. The Cabinet were very narrowly divided on it and I made a speech in which I argued that we really couldn't cut again. Harold was upset about it because he clearly intended to deflate. It was pointed out by Jim [Callaghan], quite rightly, that if you did devalue, you would also have to deflate, so you couldn't escape the package but there would be a chink of light. Otherwise, he said, it was like going along the same dark tunnel for ever. There was a break for a few minutes in the middle of Cabinet and Harold said he was glad the meeting had gone against devaluation as he himself would have to consider his position if it had gone in favour.

[27 July] To the National Executive this morning and we started with a discussion of the recent economic measures. Harold explained what had happened and why and then we had Jim Callaghan and George. There was a host of criticisms from the trade union members. Jack Jones[8] was absolutely opposed to what had been done and made it clear that the TGWU was not prepared to support the Government.... I have never felt a more fundamentally hostile atmosphere from the trade union side. Hardly any of the constituency people spoke at all and the battle was fought entirely between the three leading members of the Cabinet and the trade union leaders.

Tony Benn, *Out of the Wilderness. Diaries, 1963–67*, edited by Ruth Winstone, London, 1988, pp. 455, 456–7, 457–8, 460–1.

3.10   The decline of Party organisation

By deflating the economy, the government hit working-class living standards. This was the reverse of what Labour members had hoped for. Some responded by leaving the Party; others abstained from activity. This trend is illustrated in the case of the Party in Newton Heath ward, an industrial district of Manchester. Recorded attendances at meetings indicate the extent to which numbers declined.

Month of Meeting	Attendance	Other Information
7.65	28	
9.65	17	
10.65	40	
11.65	33	average attendance in 1965: 30
1.66	24	
2.66	33	
3.66	32	
4.66	33	
5.66	22	
6.66	24	
7.66	30	
9.66	30	total membership: 280
10.66	33	
11.66	24	average attendance in 1966: 25
1.67	28	
2.67	23	
3.67	16	
4.67	21	
5.67	23	
6.67	24	
7.67	24	
9.67	16	
10.67	20	
12.67	15	average attendance in 1967: 18

[*Continued opposite*]

1.68	11	
2.68	10	
3.68	10	
7.68	7	
9.68	10	
10.68	6	
11.68	8	
12.68	10	average attendance in 1968: 9
1.69	19	
2.69	13	
3.69	11	
7.69	20	total membership: 109
10.69	10	total membership: 112
11.69	28	
12.69	9	average attendance in 1969: 16
1.70	11	
2.70	13	
3.70	11	
7.70	8	
9.70	8	
10.70	11	total membership: 120
11.70	22	
12.70	7	average attendance in 1970: 11

Manchester Central Reference Library, Local Studies, M147/1, Newton Heath ward minute book, 1965–71.

3.11 A demotivated Party?

Members in Birmingham, as elsewhere, were disenchanted with their leaders. As with other CLPs in the city, members in Northfield – where thousands of 'affluent workers' were employed in car production – were less willing to participate in Labour affairs than they once had been. Yet, as these reports from the constituency's four ward parties show, the picture was not all doom and gloom. Some wards remained fairly active and were well prepared for the forthcoming round of local elections; others undeniably suffered from increasing apathy.

a) *Kings Norton:*

The Secretary stated that the candidate Mr. Fred Grattidge and his agent Mr F. Willock were doing an excellent job, and that the Advice Bureau that they had recently started was attracting a number of customers....

A special meeting held at the Breedon Cross [*sic*] had been addressed by Mr. D. Faraday, but the attendance had been poor. Mr D. Bennett had spoken at the ward meeting in January when his subject had been banking.

b) *Longbridge:*

Mr. Banting reported that Alderman Sir Frank Price had spoken at the November Ward Meeting. No meeting had been held in December. Several [ward] EC meetings had been cancelled because of poor attendances, and there appeared to be some apathy in the ward....

c) *Northfield:*

Mr Elkington commented on the general feeling of apathy within the ward. Small attendances were being recorded at meetings, even though speakers had been arranged....

d) *Weoley:*

Mr Charlton reported that ward meetings were being held as political discussions and speakers were being arranged to talk on both political and non-political subjects. There had been a fund-raising programme, and both bazaars and jumble sales had been very successful.... A Supper Club had been formed.... It was also planned to hold Wine and Cheese Parties in Members' houses to raise funds. A Study Group had been formed to produce electoral material – such as the leaflet on leasehold reform.

Birmingham Public Library, Northfield Constituency Labour Party papers, General Management Committee minutes, 1968–73: minute for 22 January 1968.

3.12 Immigration: members debate the issue

The Labour government faced a dilemma over black Commonwealth immigration, an issue of increasing importance in the 1960s. One of Gaitskell's additions to clause iv committed Labour to oppose racial prejudice. In practice, however, many white Labour members shared a hostility to black people evident in the rest of British society. This discussion on race relations, recorded in the minutes of the Bedford CLP, reveals a clear difference of opinion.

A member said that we might just as well give the whole damn country to the Blacks as they would get it in the end anyway. Before long we would have a Black king on the throne and then it would be God help us! The poor old white man might just as well emigrate and leave the place to them.

He said that this Black menace had ruined our towns and forced the whites out of them. The best thing we could do would be to send the whole damn lot back to where they came from!

Mr Storrow said he was not aware that Ian Smith[9] was present but apparently he was....

Mr Whittle said they must learn to reject some of their ways. Some of them would gladly do without education for their children and street lighting, etc if it saved them paying Rates and Taxes. We were gradually winning the battle but it was a long fight....

Mr Bell said he didn't see why we should accept their ways as it was our country.

Mr Blair said they worked well along side us. But he believed in the old saying of when in Rome do as Rome does.

Dr Tombs concluded by thanking everyone for an interesting discussion.

BLPES, Bedford Divisional Labour Party, 1/12, General Management Committee minutes: minute for 12 October 1967.

3.13   Immigration: the triumph of pragmatism

In 1968 the Commons voted on the Commonwealth Immigrants Bill, an emergency measure to restrict the entry of Kenyan Asians holding British passports, keen to escape persecution in Africa. This was, despite claims to the contrary, intended to alleviate the misgivings of the white population, stoked up by the speeches of the Conservative Enoch Powell. In his autobiography David Owen,[10] at the time a junior defence minister, described how he came to vote for the measure along with the vast majority of Labour MPs.

I agonized as to how to vote. Too often we just voted like sheep. The House dividing ritually along purely party lines. On this bill I felt I would take my own decision; it was undoubtedly racial in character but perhaps it had to be racial since it was dealing with deep-seated racial prejudice in Britain.... I was never tempted to abstain since I felt this was a cop-out. I forced myself to ask what would happen if the immigration continued, as it undoubtedly would, at these levels for a few more months. What would happen in the areas of highest immigration? The answer, I felt, was violence, for the tensions in these areas was mounting. It would put an intolerable strain on race relations. This was a vote with a straight choice. Continuing with no controls or legislating to slow the rate of immigration. Principle dictated continuing, prudence indicated slowing.... I listened to every word of the debate and found myself being moved by speakers on both sides of the argument, particularly Dingle Foot, Labour MP for Ipswich, who was against the bill in principle, and Renee Short, Labour MP for Wolverhampton North-East, who was in favour and spoke of the housing, education and employment problems that her constituents currently faced. I was very upset when David Ennals, winding up the debate, tried to defend the legislation, claiming that it was not racial. I felt, by admitting what we all knew, that Britain was riddled with racial prejudice, we would get on top of prejudice and root it out. Only if we accepted the charge of institutionalized racialism would we be able to improve race relations in those urban centres where Asian immigrants were concentrated. As ten o'clock approached, I had to decide. With a heavy heart I voted for the bill.

David Owen, *Time to Declare*, Harmondsworth, 1992, pp. 112–13.

3.14 A union member resigns

Problems over economic policy remained central to Labour's declining support. Many trade unionists complained that workers were making all the sacrifices, through government attempts to control wages. In protest, one union stalwart resigned from the Stalybridge and Hyde Labour party, outlining his reasons in the local press.

I have been a full-time agent for the Labour Party and I have conducted two Parliamentary elections in my present constituency. But I can no longer work for the return of this Labour Government.

I have sent in my Labour Party membership card (paid up, as it was) with my resignation.

What is more, I shall work within my trade union (N.U.P.E. [National Union of Public Employees]) to secure its disaffiliation from the Labour Party.

When only 23 Labour M.P.s can be found to oppose the penal clauses of the prices and wages legislation, what hope have we for Socialism from the Parliamentary Labour Party, let alone this Government?

To turn the clock of history back nearly 100 years – why I should have been surprised to find 23 Labour M.P.s *supporting* such a measure.

Tameside Local Studies, DD55/2, Stalybridge and Hyde Constituency Labour Party papers, constituency secretary's correspondence, October 1967 – June 1970, news clipping dated 30 July 1968.

3.15 'In Place of Strife'

By the end of 1968 Wilson was concerned that the prevalence of strikes was damaging Labour politically and the country economically. Barbara Castle was the minister responsible for industrial relations. Taking some of the ideas in the recently published Donovan report, she sought to reduce industrial conflict in a 'socialist' manner. Thus, she drafted a white paper, entitled 'In Place of Strife', which extended unions' rights at the workplace in exchange for their acceptance of measures which would restrict unofficial strike activity. Castle's initiative exacerbated government–union tensions and, in the face of resistance from the Trades

Union Congress (TUC), she backed down. Excerpts from Castle's diary show her awareness of the promise and risk of her proposals – and the extent to which she felt let down by colleagues on both the right and left.

[4 December 1968] ... went to see Harold. He had just read the first draft of our White Paper and was quite lyrical. He said we had obviously done a first-class job and a lot of hard work. 'As I said to Marcia [Williams], Barbara has not so much out-heathed Heath as outflanked him.'...

[7 January 1969] ... I'm under no illusions that Donovan may be the political end of me with our own people. I'm taking a terrific gamble and there is absolutely no certainty that it will pay off. My only comfort is that I am proposing something I believe in. I see no objection in principle to asking the trade union movement to adapt itself to changing circumstances and my one aim is to strengthen it. One doesn't do that by clinging to things as they are.

[7 May] ... I pointed out to them [a group of backbench Labour MPs] that there were as many views about my Bill in the room as there were people. If we were the Cabinet, we would be disagreeing passionately. Yet in the end we would have to cohere around *some* view, even if we marginally disagreed with it. The trouble with the PLP, I told them, was that it would now only cohere *against* the Government. But the credibility of some of us was at stake. As Mendes-France had said, 'To govern is to choose.' Yet they were running away from choices. And I told Mike [Foot] flatly that he had grown soft on a diet of soft options because he never had to choose.

[17 June] The most traumatic day of my political life. Any hope that the TUC's intransigence would have hardened the attitude of the inner Cabinet soon disappeared and we had to go into Cabinet disunited and unprepared....

At 4.30 Harold was still in as buoyant mood as I have ever seen him. He is clearly determined to resign on this if necessary, but will go down fighting, probably believing that, if he fights, he will win....

Roy [Jenkins] sat silent through all this looking pretty worried. Before the resumed meeting he had sent a message asking me to come to his room at 4 pm. There he told me, with that evasive look he has been developing lately, that I would have gathered that he no longer thought that the fight was worth the cost.

Barbara Castle, *The Castle Diaries, 1964–76*, London, 1990, pp. 284, 296, 328, 342–3.

3.16 Back from the brink

> Castle considered the rejection of 'In Place of Strife' a lost opportunity. As this excerpt from a Labour paper distributed in the south-east of England shows, others in the Party were glad she had failed. They called on the government to stop attacking trade unions and start supporting them.

Sanity has prevailed at last.

The Government and the T.U.C. has seemed set on a collision course until the very last minute. What would have been the result if a solution had not been reached?

It would not be overstating to say that it would not only have brought down this present Labour administration but would have alienated the trade union movement and broken for ever the Labour Party as we know it today.

Mr. Wilson should learn a lesson from this problem; whilst all governments must legislate for the good of the community as a whole, they must never forget that the people who voted for them did so for one reason only. Because they believed in the same ideals.

Trade unionists, Co-operators and Socialists band together with one interest: in order that collectively they may change society to make it better for all.

A large proportion of this movement has to work for its very existence in a society which has the odds stacked in the favour of the employers. The only effective weapon the trades unions have is the right to withhold their labour.

In spite of what the Press may say, this right to strike is used sparingly.

To take this right away or to emasculate it until it has no real significance is not a breakthrough in industrial relations. It is reducing still more the limited powers of the ordinary worker.

The T.U.C. is a responsible body; it may move slowly but it does represent the major, albeit underprivileged, sector of industry.

It may well be that in future years the T.U.C. will have to negotiate not only with employers but with a right wing, authoritarian government only too eager to use the powers which the government first envisaged.

That situation has now been averted. The next step must be to ensure this last minute agreement works.

The long term aim is to build upon the agreement and see that in unity the Labour movement makes up the lost ground and returns the government for a third consecutive term of office.

LPA, Local Party Papers Collection, *Surrey and Middlesex Clarion*, July 1969.

3.17   Disaffection on the right

Whilst criticised by the Party's left as well as trade unionists, Wilson's government did not escape attack from the right. The MP Christopher Mayhew, who defected to the Liberals in 1974, was one of a number of MPs frustrated by their Party's trade union connection and reliance upon working-class votes. In 1969 he wrote a study of the Party that anticipated many of the arguments of those who later formed the SDP.

It was natural enough in those days [the 1930s] to stress the rights of wage-earners and soft-pedal their obligations: they contributed so much more to society than they received in return. But a lot has changed since then, and it could be argued nowadays that working-class power is less an instrument of social justice than a means by which one section of the workers promotes its own interests at the expense of others....

During the 1968 railway strike, I gave a lift in my car to two elderly wage-earning women – not Labour members – who were struggling to get to work in central London. They were bitter critics of the National Union of Railwaymen, and I felt it strange that my Party should be supported and financed not by them but by the strikers. We seemed to have travelled too far from our original idea of Socialism, based on co-operation, neighbourliness and readiness to help other people.

Many working-class people also show Conservative attitudes over a large range of contemporary issues ... it seems clear that on subjects such as race and colour, internationalism, homosexuality, abortion, divorce, capital punishment and flogging, working-class people tend to take a more traditional view than middle and upper-class people. The Labour Party, whose political ideas are essentially radical, nevertheless gets most of its support from some of the least radical sections of society.

There is also this further awkward paradox. We aim rightly at the creation of a classless society: but how far can this be achieved by a party which in practice gets its main support from a particular class? The Labour movement organises citizens not according to religion, sex, occupation, region or temperament, but predominantly as wage-earners, members of trade unions and co-operative organisations. May we not, by the manner in which we attempt to destroy class, make people more conscious of it and to that extent help it to survive?

Christopher Mayhew, *Party Games*, London, 1969, pp. 94–5.

3.18 The 1964–70 governments: Wilson's assessment

In the introduction to his 1971 account of the 1964–70 governments, Harold Wilson looked for extenuating circumstances for their many shortcomings. These he found in the field of economics. Wilson suggested that had Labour been re-elected in 1970 he would have implemented many of the reforms so cruelly postponed whilst he had tackled the country's economic problems.

This book is the record of a Government all but a year of whose life was dominated by an inherited balance of payments problem which was nearing a crisis at the moment we took office; we lived and governed during a period when that problem made frenetic speculative attack on Britain both easy and profitable....

Yet, looking back from today, the detached observer might agree that Britain and Britain's Government, working together, had transformed a crippling deficit into one of the strongest balance of payments surpluses in the world. The sneers abroad about Britain's sickness had given place to admiration. Nor could this transformation have been brought about by reliance on the drift or the weak surrender to blind market forces which had characterized the years of our predecessors. It had meant the application of specifically socialist measures, some of them newly designed for the problems we were facing, to secure national policies in industry and a more purposive use of our national resources for overcoming a national malady. It had meant, equally, through our social policies – including taxation and greater public expenditure – the creation of a fairer order of society, without which we could not appeal, with any hope of success, for the sacrifices, restraint and efforts which were necessary from a united people, and which alone made possible the achievement of a situation of national strength.

It was a Government which had faced disappointment after disappointment, and none greater than the economic restraints on our ability to carry through the social revolution to which we were committed at the speed we would have wished. Yet, despite those restraints and the need to transfer resources from domestic expenditure, private and public, to the needs of our export markets, we carried through an expansion in the social services, health, welfare and housing, education and social security, unparalleled in our history.

... If in all these things we had not gone as far as we would have wished, we achieved far more than most would have expected. As we went forward for a mandate to continue what we had begun, we were determined to use our newly developed economic strength as a basis for faster economic expansion, based on full employment, and for a more rapid rate of improvement in the welfare service.

In the event, we were denied that mandate; once again, a Labour Government was prevented from building on the foundations which it had laid.

Harold Wilson, *The Labour Government 1964–70. A Personal Record*, Harmondsworth, 1974, pp. 17–18.

3.19   The 1964–70 governments: the left's assessment

Ernie Roberts became an MP in 1979. During the 1960s he was a national official of the Amalgamated Engineering Union who was famous for his support of left-wing causes. Like most other Labour activists, he took a less than sympathetic view of the Wilson government. This he made clear in his memoirs.

The Labour Government which was elected in 1964 worked on a shoestring of votes, tailoring its policy to suit its tiny majority. Re-elected in 1966 with a three-figure majority, the Wilson Government proceeded to jump with both feet into the job of making capitalism work better. Old Tory policies, dusted and polished were brought out to serve a Labour administration, and Labour's left – both in parliament and out of it – were incensed at this misuse of their Party. For Government backbenchers life was made especially difficult, as they were reduced to lobby-fodder, expected to march through the right lobby (and it was 'right' in both senses of the word) when it came to a vote, and their position recalled the words of W. S. Gilbert in 'Iolanthe':

When in that House M.P.s divide
If they've got a brain and a cerebellum too,
They've got to leave that brain outside
And vote just as their leaders tell 'em to.

Harold Wilson reinforced this when he reminded 'his' back-benchers that they could have their licences revoked like dogs if they stepped out of line.

The period 1966–70 was a time of despondency throughout the country, as the electorate saw a Government which it had elected with something approaching euphoria in 1966 gradually sliding down a miserable slope towards wage-freeze and depression. For Labour Party members who really believed in Clause 4 of the constitution, this period was one of misery and frustration.

Ernie Roberts, *Strike Back*, Orpington, 1994, p. 187.

4

Decade of discontent: the 1970s

The 1970s was a decade in which Labour's fraught relationship with the trade unions became vital to the Party's fate. Harold Wilson left office facing the accusation that his government had worked against trade union interests. This led to calls for the unions to be granted a central place within Party policy making. The result of this was the 'social contract', which formed the basis of the Party's 1974 manifesto and – formally at least – the strategy of the subsequent Labour governments. These administrations faced economic problems more acute even than those confronted by Labour governments in the 1960s, and to stabilise the situation they fell back on the latter's remedy: pay restraint. Workers were reluctant adherents to this policy and their opposition culminated in what was known as the 'winter of discontent'. Another feature of the Party during this period was increasing disagreement over economic policy. After 1970 pressure was renewed to increase state control. Despite agreeing to this in opposition, once in power the leadership avoided most of their previous commitments. By 1979 activists' frustration with their leaders echoed the hostility of union members to further wage control.

4.1 The need to support trade unionism

Once out of office, the Labour leadership was urged to repair the damage done to the Party's union link. The need to oppose Conservative industrial relations legislation and support striking workers, such as the miners, was emphasised by some. In this speech to the 1970 Party conference, the MP Stan Orme[1] made this point emphatically.

In Parliament during the last four or five years some of us have had a very traumatic experience, it has been like an industrial seminar. Everybody, of course, that took part in it has not

92

necessarily worked in industry, but they had a lot to say about it. I hope that is now over and finished.

I hope that the Tory Mark II Industrial Relations Bill[2] is going to be fought hard, but I hope there is going to be no resurrection of the Labour Industrial Relations Bill Mark I [i.e. 'In Place of Strife']. I hope nobody is going to say, 'Income's Policy is dead, long live the income's policy,' as the Movement will have none of it....

I do not know what Barbara [Castle] is going to say in reply to this debate.... But I would say this to Barbara, that in all fairness to the Party she will have to reject her past policies if she is going to fight the present policies (*Applause.*) If Barbara is going to be credible in the House of Commons it will be farewell to the past policies and an absolute unanimous fight against the present Tory Government at the present time.

I believe that we meet at this Conference following a defeat on 18 June, a sad occasion for everybody in this hall, and one many of us would have described, in much of our industrial policy in the past, as having some basis in that defeat. But now we should be turning away, it should not be a division between the Trade Union Movement and the Labour Party or the Parliamentary Labour Party, we must be shoulder to shoulder with the miners, and I urge the miners to vote 100 per cent for strike action (*Applause.*)

I would say to the miners, by a quirk of history you have been thrust in the forefront once more, we will not turn our backs upon you, the Labour Movement will not pass by on the other side. Vote for strike action, let the Labour Movement stand firm behind the miners and behind all industrial workers that are fighting for a fair and just wage. This is all they are asking. Let us see the Labour Movement support them to the hilt.

Report of the Sixty-Ninth Annual Conference of the Labour Party, London, 1970, p. 119.

4.2 Halifax speaks

As Orme hoped, opposing the Conservative government's Industrial Relations Act brought Party and unions together. Given that 'In Place of Strife' was similar to the Conservative legislation, Wilson's motives in opposing the Act were questionable. However, as the wording of a resolution passed by Halifax CLP indicates, activists rejected the Heath government's measures with a clear conscience.

Mr T. Enright, in a vigorous speech, exposed the threat presented to the Trade Unions, working people generally, and the foundations of democracy by the Government's Industrial Relations Bill....

The motion being put was carried unanimously and it was *resolved* that

This General Management Committee speaking in the name of the Halifax Constituency Labour Party, declares that it is totally opposed to the Industrial Relations Bill. It believes that the proposed legal sanctions would be a backward step, damaging not only to the Trade Union movement but also to democracy itself. British liberties rest on the bed rock of free Trade Unions. Believing thus, the Halifax Constituency Labour Party declares its intention to resist and repel this vicious attack on the working people by all constitutional means at its command.

Halifax Public Library, Calderdale Archives, TU 28/6, Halifax Constituency Labour Party Executive Committee and General Management Committee Minute Book, 1970–71: minute for 21 January 1971.

4.3   The left's agenda

The left's response to the Wilson governments' inability to promote growth was to renew the call for more direct control of the economy. It was believed that only this would overcome the country's profound problems and so help produce the wealth necessary to eradicate poverty. Moreover, in this 'socialist' economic transformation, the unions would play a central role – unlike in 1964–70. One of the most influential works to make this point was the MP Stuart Holland's *The Socialist Challenge*.[3]

The main dimensions of Labour's socialist challenge include not only a penetration of the commanding heights of modern capitalism ... but also a simultaneous transformation of the prevailing class structures which concentrate economic and social power in the hands of a largely self-perpetuating oligarchy....

As is argued throughout this work, progress to socialism would be an on-going process, but one in which the critical centres of capitalist power and class were transformed by a socialist government, backed by the trade unions. It is a key premise of this analysis that such transformation can be achieved through democratic processes ... such democratic reforms must be effectively revolutionary in character. In other words, they must reverse the present dominance of capitalist modes of production and capitalist motivation into a dominance of a democratically controlled socialism. They must transform capitalist society rather than try ineffectively to alleviate its implicit injustice.

... It will only be through the negotiated and bargained support of the trade union movement that such critical change will prove to be possible. If it is also to be effective, such bargaining and such negotiation must involve a new dimension to the relationship between the Labour party and the Labour movement, backed by a new means of widening the effective control of working people over the main strategy for social and economic transformation. This means not only a social contract in the sense of agreement on the main strategy for transformation of British capitalism, negotiated between government and the unions at the national level, but also a spearheading of means for working people either to control their own companies outright, or to take part in a process of national bargaining on the contribution which their firms should make both to themselves and to society as a whole.

Stuart Holland, *The Socialist Challenge*, London, 1975, pp. 36–8.

4.4   The Labour government's 'fresh approach'

The February 1974 general election was held during what the Labour manifesto described as 'the most serious political and economic crisis since 1945'. This document was the product of close consultation with a number of influential trade union leaders. It outlined the Party's 'fresh approach', which entailed 'an entirely new recognition of

the claim of social justice', in particular price controls and a
severe wealth tax.

These measures affecting prices and taxation policy will prove by
deeds the determination of the new Labour Government to set
Britain on the road towards a new social and economic equality.
After so many failures in the field of incomes policy – under the
Labour Government but even more seriously under the Tory
Government's compulsory wage controls – only deeds can
persuade. Only practical action by the Government to create a
much fairer distribution of the national wealth can convince the
worker and his family and his trade union that 'an incomes
policy' is not some kind of trick to force him, particularly if he
works in a public service or nationalised industry, to bear the
brunt of the national burden. But as it is proved that the
Government is ready to act – against high prices, rents and other
impositions falling most heavily on the low paid and on
pensioners – so we believe that the trade unions *voluntarily*
(which is the only way it can be done for any period in a free
society), will co-operate to make the whole policy successful. We
believe that the action we propose on prices, together with an
understanding with the TUC on the lines which we have already
agreed, will create the right economic climate for money incomes
to grow in line with production. That is the essence of the new
social contract which the Labour Party has discussed at length
and agreed with the TUC and which must take its place as a
central feature of the new economic policy of a Labour
Government....

The aims set out in this manifesto are Socialist aims, and are
proud of the word. It is only by setting our aims high, even amid
the hazards of our present economic situation, that the idealism
and high intelligence, especially of our young people, can be
enlisted. It is indeed our intention to:

a. Bring about a fundamental and irreversible shift in the balance
of power and wealth in favour of working people and their families;

b. Eliminate poverty wherever it exists in Britain, and commit
ourselves to a substantial increase in our contribution to fight
poverty abroad;

c. Make power in industry genuinely accountable to the
workers and the community at large;

d. Achieve far greater economic equality – in income, wealth and living standards;

e. Increase social equality by giving far greater importance to full employment, housing, education and social benefits;

f. Improve the environment in which our people live and work and spend their leisure.

Let Us Work Together. Labour's Way Out of the Crisis. The Labour Party Manifesto 1974, London, 1974, pp. 9–10, 14–15.

4.5   Optimism amongst the entryists

In writing a report of his branch's activities during 1974, the secretary of Putney's Young Socialists (YS) gave evidence of his Trotskyist beliefs. Whether he was a member of Militant or any other entryist body is open to doubt. Even so, his optimism with regard to the future is unlikely to have been shared by many in the cabinet.

By no means are we pessimistic about the future, in fact we are supremely optimistic that in a year's time we will be a flourishing branch.

The reason for our optimism is based on the deepening crisis of British capitalism reflected in the impossible position of the Labour Government. As we warned at the time of the election unless the Government implements socialist policies then they will be forced to carry out the demands of the C.B.I. [Confederation of British Industry]. Already, this has been borne out, on more than one occasion, after only three months of majority government.

It is the perspective of enormous class struggles, of the inevitable formation of a National Government,[4] of the continuous leftward swing in the Labour Party itself which gives Y.S. comrades confidence that young workers will turn to us for the only solution – the socialist solution – to the problems they face, which are the problems faced by the working class as a whole.

BLPES, Hugh Jenkins' papers, 3/3, *Putney Labour Party Annual Report 1974*.

4.6 Early difficulties over the 'social contract'

Jack Jones, general secretary of the TGWU, was the main architect of the set of policies known as the 'social contract'. As he reveals in his autobiography, union and cabinet differences of interpretation over the purpose of the contract were exposed soon after Labour had regained power.

By early 1975 the Social Contract was under severe attack. Harold Wilson and Denis Healey[5] did not seem happy at the co-operation they were receiving from the trade unions and there was strong criticism of the Government in our ranks because of their inability to stem the rapidly rising tide of unemployment and inflation. I never doubted the value of the Social Contract, which I saw as a major step towards economic equality and better conditions for working people, and used every democratic means to gain the co-operation of fellow trade unionists. Sometimes I felt that political leaders did not appreciate the hard work involved in influencing rank-and-file opinion.

Carping criticism of trade union activities by Harold Wilson and Denis Healey had not helped, and at a meeting of the Liaison Committee I appealed to them to appreciate the constructive work being done. Len Murray[6] was constrained to say that wage restraint was not the 'be all and end all', and presented the TUC case for more emphasis on investment and productivity in solving the economic problems of the country....

The Annual Congress of the Scottish TUC took place at Aberdeen in April 1975.... In the course of my speech I said: 'My appeal is to respect the Social Contract, and to support it. To do this would mean advancing the interests of our members and keeping a Labour Government in power. Can we really afford to let this Government be thrown out? The Labour Government, for all its limitations, is two hundred times better than a Tory Government.' I added that the Social Contract was one means of laying down the policy on which the Government would move. 'How else but with unity between the trade unions and the Labour Government are we going to fight rising unemployment and the redundancies that are taking place?'

Jack Jones, *Union Man*, London, 1986, p. 295.

4.7 The 'social contract' and the unions

In 1975, Ron Hayward, general secretary of the Labour Party, addressed a Scottish miners' gala on the subject of the 'social contract'. In this speech he emphasised the government's radical policies but stressed the extent to which they depended upon the cooperation of the unions. By cooperation Hayward meant voluntary wage restraint. In the event, the government delivered few of the policies promised by Hayward whilst union cooperation was, at best, limited.

... the Government must continue to pursue its objectives of controlling the giant manufacturing and oil concerns, and ... [fulfil] Labour's social objectives such as the reduction of inequalities in income and wealth, the public ownership of development land, and the ending of selection in education and the abolition of direct grant schools. For it is by these tests that the Government will be judged – not only by the Labour Movement but by the nation as a whole.

This is not to say that carrying out our Manifesto is going to be easy, given the present economic situation. The Chancellor's job is always a bed of nails – and Denis Healey's task is no exception. The clear danger now is that the inflationary surge will further limit our room for manoeuvre. For massive increases in personal spending and in the costs of providing essential services are bound to cut the amount which can be afforded to finance future investment and social programmes. This is why the Party and the Trade Unions must unite to defend the social wage. And that is why the Social Contract must be strengthened and clarified. We cannot finance the present level of consumption and at the same time finance all our social policies; we have to make sure that the old, the weak, the young, the handicapped and the homeless are not the victims of this vicious cycle of inflation. This issue is absolutely crucial – the Government's very survival is staked upon it. The way forward is through the Social Contract.

Voluntary co-operation is really the only philosophy that can work in this country. It is the only way we can unite society while ensuring that working people and their families do not lose out. A return to the traditional remedies – favoured as usual by the Tories – of compulsory wage control and unemployment would, I believe, cause all the old antagonisms and hatreds to re-emerge. Our task is to unite the nation – and compulsion on wages and mass unemployment, can only serve to disunite.

The Miners have always held a high position in the loyalty and comradeship of the Labour Movement. Twice in recent years the whole Labour Movement has united in your defence against those who sought to divide and rule. Now is the time to remember our obligations and responsibilities to each other and to the wider unity of the Movement of which we are part. Only by uniting behind the Social Contract have we any chance of carrying out our Manifesto and creating a fairer, more equal, society.

But one message I do most of all want to go out from this meeting. The Social Contract is not just about wages. It is about the whole spectrum of social, economic and industrial policies – and about the part to be played in the development of these policies by the Trade Union Movement.

It is a policy, what is more, that is based upon our promised programme of intervention in industry so as to bring about full employment in all regions of our country....

This is the way forward. A programme of action, based on democratic socialist objectives and democratic socialist principles.

The Labour Government is now proving to the nation that it has the courage of its convictions but it is necessary for all Trade Unionists to play their part and give our Government their full support.

Manchester Central Reference Library, Local Studies, Manchester Ardwick Constituency Labour Party papers, M411/Box 5100/ Transport House correspondence, January 1975–December 1976 file, press release, 14 June 1975.

4.8   The need to reduce inflation

Having had enough of trying to keep an increasingly fractious Party united in worsening economic conditions, Harold Wilson unexpectedly resigned in March 1976. In his first speech to conference as leader, James Callaghan lectured delegates on what he considered to be the new economic realities. According to Callaghan, inflation was the main enemy as it caused unemployment. Thus, tackling inflation would reduce unemployment. In his view, wage rises – supposedly the main root of inflation – had to be severely curtailed. This was not a message designed to please the unions.

The cosy world we were told would go on for ever, where full employment would be guaranteed by a stroke of the Chancellor's pen, cutting taxes, deficit spending, that cosy world is gone....

When we reject unemployment as an economic instrument – as we do – and when we reject also superficial remedies, as socialists must, then we must ask ourselves unflinchingly what is the cause of high unemployment. Quite simply and unequivocally, it is caused by paying ourselves more than the value of what we produce....

We used to think that you could spend your way out of a recession, and increase employment by cutting taxes and boosting Government spending. I tell you in all candour that option no longer exists, and that in so far as it ever did exist, it only worked on each occasion since the war by injecting a bigger dose of inflation into the economy, followed by a higher level of unemployment as the next step. Higher inflation followed by higher unemployment. We have just escaped from the highest rate of inflation this country has known; we have not yet escaped from the consequences: high unemployment....

Now we must get back to fundamentals. First, overcoming unemployment now unambiguously depends on our labour costs being at least comparable with those of our major competitors. Second, we can only become competitive by having the right kind of investment at the right kind of level, and by significantly improving the productivity of both labour and capital....

Britain is now at a watershed. We have the chance to make real and fundamental choices about priorities which are absolutely necessary to achieve a growing and prosperous manufacturing industry, with all the advantages that can follow.

Let me be quite clear. If we did not possess the Social Contract and an industrial strategy that has been agreed between the Government and employers and trade unions, with all the socialist measures that are involved in that Contract and in the industrial strategy, if we did not possess this we would have no chance of forging a powerful British economy in the next decade. But we are getting co-operation on these issues.

Report of the Seventy-Fifth Annual Conference of the Labour Party, London, 1976, pp. 188–9

4.9   Criticism of the state

In response to the government's problems, some Labour MPs went even further than Callaghan. Leading social democrats – in this case John Mackintosh – questioned their own assumptions. Crosland and Gaitskell had looked on government intervention as a means of promoting growth. By the later 1970s, however, some of their followers considered that the state was actually an impediment to economic prosperity. Here, Mackintosh reviews the ideas of Crosland's *The Future of Socialism* (document 1.12) in an essay published not long after the latter's death in 1977.

The great weakness of Crosland's position was not that he underestimated the resilience of capitalism but that he over-estimated it. Throughout the book he, like Marxists, classical economists and Keynesians, assumes that the urge driving private people is so strong that they will perform in the economic field whatever the state does to them and whatever the social atmosphere. Crosland did realise that steeply progressive taxation can have an effect on incentives and he wanted to reduce taxes on income and increase taxes on wealth. But he considered that while socialist governments might reduce and circumscribe the private sector, it would still have sufficient internal dynamic and desire to expand, to continue investing and growing.... In fact, the chief weakness in Crosland's whole position is that the mixed economy has not shown this resilience. The public sector has been demoralised by constant government intervention; and the private sector has lost all confidence because its rewards and reputation have diminished and managers have preferred to play safe, to cut production, to hold back investment, to accept union domination and restrictive practices....

A further and much more fundamental weakness of Crosland's policies was his assumption, typical of the 1950s, that growth could and would continue unabated.... He considers the impact of higher taxation on wealth on the propensity to save, but concludes that institutional pressure to save will continue unabated; and also that similar corporate desires for higher output and better performance will keep up activity and investment in the private sector despite heavy taxation and the emphasis any Labour Government must place on public expenditure. In general, he thought that private industry was sufficiently confident and resilient to provide the motor power for innovation and growth; and he saw no great problem about the efficiency of the nationalised industries.

These basic assumptions have been proved wrong.

John P. Mackintosh, 'Has social democracy failed in Britain?', *Political Quarterly*, 49, 1978, pp. 266–7.

4.10   Hostility to the 'social contract'

Most union activists opposed wage controls. The extent to which they represented the wishes of the majority of union members is, however, open to question. For example, in 1977, affiliated to Warrington Trades Council were fifty-one union branches – mainly composed of skilled or semi-skilled manual workers. These branches represented over 15,000 people; yet, on average, only forty-eight out of 149 delegates attended meetings. As the Council's annual report for 1977 indicates, those who participated in such deliberations did not like the 'social contract'.

Throughout the year the Council's opposition to the Social Contract and any form of wage restraint was maintained.

The annual general meeting endorsed unanimously the letter drafted on the instructions of the Executive Committee highly critical of Government economic strategy and the acquiescence of the General Council of the TUC.

The letter called for a change of policy to include –

... Embark on a policy of higher wages and pensions and spend more on the social services.

Impose a six months price freeze while strict price control methods are worked out.

Cut the arms bill and introduce a wealth tax, this, together with extra revenue from the expansion of the economy and the savings on unemployment and social security benefits would help wipe out the budget deficit.

The Council was represented by the Secretary at the Liaison Committee for the Defence of Trade Unions Conference held 26th February and by J. F. Wade EETPU [Electrical, Electronic, Telecommunications and Plumbing Union] Electrical Section at the National Conference for a Return to Free Collective Bargaining organised by the Leyland Combined Shop Stewards Committee and held 3rd April.

Written reports and the declaration of both Conferences were distributed to delegates and accepted by the Council. Arising from the discussion on the report of the April Conference, it was agreed that branches be notified by letter of the result of the discussion.

Only two branches made comment to that letter, namely –

The National League of the Blind and Disabled who, in the main, did not wish for a return to free collective bargaining and favoured greater co-operation with the Labour Government, and The Society of Civil and Public Servants BNFL [British Nuclear Fuels Limited] Branch, who, whilst saying that they would support a Phase III of wages policy, maintained that many of their members were opposed to a Labour Government and objected to the collaboration between most trade unions and the Labour Party.

Warrington Public Library, Local Studies Library, *Warrington District Trades Union Council. Annual Report 1977*, p. 18.

4.11   Defence of the record

In a speech delivered in November 1982 Michael Foot, by then Party leader, defended the record of the 1974–79 Labour governments in which he had played such an important part. Given the light in which these administrations were viewed, this was no easy task. By the early

1980s, they were criticised – albeit for different reasons –
by activists and MPs on both the left and right.

Two brands of revisionist history have been applied to this
period. First the Tories try to portray the Social Contract and the
whole of the 1974–79 Labour Government as a period of
disaster....

Another form of revisionist history portrays the Social Contract
as a betrayal of the labour movement and of the working class.
Mistakes and misjudgments, certainly: I would not attempt to
question that charge. But the larger and deeper charge is utterly
unfounded....

In terms of social progress, the achievement of the 1974–79
government is impressive. The protection of pensions which
increased in value by a quarter, the introduction of child benefit,
by itself one of the great reforms of the century, the employment
protection Act, the Health and Safety legislation started to offer a
transformation for many of our people. Shipbuilding and aircraft
were nationalised, and the National Enterprise Board, while
disappointing the highest expectations, still offered solid
advances....

Major advances were made in the security of people's
livelihood, of pensioners, of people in work and perhaps, in
retrospect, most strikingly in the position of women. The first
stage of equal pay, child benefit, sex discrimination legislation
and employment protection laid the foundation for transforming
the position of women in our society....

The policy also, let me remind you, was successful in reducing
inflation....

However, ... any policy which culminated in the election of the
present government cannot be regarded as a success. It must also
be admitted that by 1977, while there was still a large measure of
support for the policy, there was also substantial opposition
especially within the labour movement.

All governments must modify their programmes according to
circumstances, and of course there are always people ready to
denounce such modifications as betrayals. Such modifications
began fairly soon after the 1974 election. The decision to make
planning agreements voluntary rather than compulsory was taken
in mid-1974. The process of reducing public sector borrowing

and reducing company taxation began at the end of 1974. By mid-1975 this process was adding to inflation through increased indirect taxes and subsidies.

Nevertheless ... there was a bigger change in 1976. It was not however the failure to sustain 'the government side of the bargain' which led to the final collapse of the bargain. While the TUC regularly drew attention in their documents to their concern over such matters as planning, import controls, and unemployment, the breakdown actually occurred over pay.

New Statesman, 26 November 1982.

4.12   The 'winter of discontent'

The final 'breakdown ... over pay' occurred during the winter of 1978–79, known as the 'winter of discontent'. According to James Callaghan's account, this was the most significant cause of Labour's 1979 defeat. In his eyes, the government had improved the country's economic position and had reasonable hopes of retaining office. However, Callaghan's attempt to impose a 5 per cent limit on wage increases created problems. Most workers and employers in the private sector ignored his prohibition in a series of spectacular settlements during the autumn of 1978. In the public sector, where many of the lowest paid were concentrated, the government was determined to reject any increases which breached its pay norm. The scene was set for conflict.

The contagion spread to other industries and services, and during January 1979 unofficial strikes erupted every week, with workers in one industry inflicting hardship on their fellows in other industries. Public service workers were in the van. Some union officials did nothing to discourage them.... Even with the passage of time I find it painful to write about some of the excesses that took place. One of the most notorious was the refusal of Liverpool grave-diggers to bury the dead, accounts of which appalled the country when they saw pictures of mourners being turned away from the cemetery. Such heartlessness and cold-blooded indifference to the feelings of families at moments of intense grief rightly aroused deep revulsion and did further untold harm to the cause of trade unionism that I, like many others, had been proud to defend throughout my life. What would the men of Tolpuddle have said? My own anger increased when I learned that the Home Secretary Merlyn Rees had called upon Alan Fisher, the General Secretary of NUPE, to use his influence to get the grave-diggers to go back to work, and Fisher had refused.

... Both the Labour Government and the trade unions had become widely unpopular. It was but the latest demonstration of a truth we have all uttered to the effect that the fortunes of the unions and the Labour Party cannot be separated. As one trade union leader told his colleagues during the worst of our troubles, 'The TUC can either have a Labour Government with some unpalatable policies, or a Conservative Government with disastrous ones.' The serious and widespread industrial dislocation caused by the strikes of January 1979, short-lived though they were, sent the Government's fortunes cascading downhill, our loss of authority in one field leading to misfortune in others just as an avalanche, gathering speed, sweeps all before it.

James Callaghan, *Time and Chance*, London, 1987, pp. 537, 540.

4.13   Defeat over devolution

> Ironically, given all its problems with the economy and the unions, the Callaghan government was finally brought down by another issue entirely: the failure to devolve power from Westminster to Scotland and Wales. The Scottish Labour MP Willie Hamilton takes up this story, which concludes with Callaghan obliged to call a general election.

The Labour Party had been frightened by the surge of support for the Scottish Nationalists in the 1974 autumn Election, when the SNP [Scottish Nationalist Party] took 30 per cent of the vote [in Scotland], only a few percentage points behind Labour, who had 36 per cent, and well ahead of the Tories, who had 24.7 per cent. Only a small switch from Labour to the SNP could have meant disaster for us in the Labour Party....

In consequence, the Labour Party found itself committed to the creation of a Scottish Assembly, not out of a conviction that it was *right*, but that it was *expedient*, a simple case of self-preservation.... I didn't like my Government caving in to the ravings of the Scottish Nationalists. I was lukewarm to the whole idea of a Scottish Parliament, so when the Government produced its bill, I supported the idea of a *consultative* referendum for the Scottish people, and I also thought it reasonable to insist that 40 per cent should be shown to support the concept of a Scottish Assembly. In the end, that target was not reached. The SNP Members of Parliament were furious, and tabled a Motion of No Confidence in the Government. The debate on that motion on 28 March was one of great excitement and emotion. When the vote was declared, the Motion had been won by a majority of *one*, and the very next day Jim Callaghan announced there would be a General Election on 3 May.

Willie Hamilton, *Blood on the Walls*, London, 1992, pp. 145–6.

4.14   The leader against the Party

After announcing the date of the election, Callaghan turned his attention to Labour's manifesto. He was faced with a number of policies endorsed by conference which he considered unacceptable. Tony Benn and other representatives of the NEC were keen to ensure that the will of conference was expressed in the manifesto. Callaghan possessed the leader's veto and used it, despite Benn's protests. Here Benn records the discussion over the abolition of the House of Lords. His entry made after the manifesto had been published showed that, although they had lost the battle, if Labour failed to win re-election, the left was determined to continue the war.

[2 April 1979] We came to the House of Lords, and I said that the Party had believed for a long time, and it was unanimously accepted at Conference, that the Lords held back our legislation, there was too much patronage and we should state that.

Jim said, 'I won't have it, I won't have it.'

Eric [Heffer][7] lost his temper and banged the table. 'What do you mean you won't have it? Who are you to dictate? Who do you think you are? You are just a member of the Party.' He banged the table again.

'Well,' said Jim, 'I won't have it.'

I said, 'You can't do that.'

'I can.'

'No you can't. What are we to say to people who joined the Labour Party to have some influence on our parliamentary system? They will say, "We joined the Party, we got this through, we've elected a Labour MP and we want him to implement our policy."'

Jim said, 'You'll have to change the Leader.'

I said, 'That's making it into a personality issue, not a political issue at all.'

'Well, I won't do it. I am Leader of the Party and I have to decide what is right. I have responsibilities that I have to take and I won't do it.'

[7 April] The papers today described the manifesto meeting as a triumph for Jim over the left and me. If we do lose the Election, no one can say we lost it by forcing through a more radical manifesto than Jim wanted. But the battle to democratise the Party has to start now.

Tony Benn, *Conflicts of Interest. Diaries 1977–80*, edited by Ruth Winstone, London, 1990, pp. 482, 488.

5

Civil war, 1979–83

Loss of power in 1979 exposed the parliamentary leadership to severe criticism from the rest of the Party. On the left, the 1974–79 governments' failure to implement those 'socialist' measures contained in the February 1974 manifesto was seen to be the most important cause of defeat. From this perspective, more internal democracy was necessary if this situation was not to recur. Such analysis was rejected by most MPs. They saw internal reform as increasing the influence of activists – some of whom were entryists – who favoured electorally unpopular policies. For a time, united behind Tony Benn, and enjoying the unprecedented support of major trade unions, the left appeared unstoppable.

5.1   The unions criticised

The 'winter of discontent' brought to a head the mutual disaffection between the leadership of the Party and of the trade unions. This sentiment intensified after 1979 as many union leaders used their conference block votes to support critics of the 1974–79 governments. In his autobiography Denis Healey echoed the opinion of some that union 'extremists' – not the governments' record – were the cause of all the Party's subsequent problems.

The Winter of Discontent was not caused by the frustration of ordinary workers after a long period of wage restraint. It was caused by institutional pressures from local trade union activists who had found their roles severely limited by three years of income policy agreed by their national leaders....

Unfortunately the Labour Party's financial and constitutional links with the unions made it difficult for us to draw too much attention to their role in our defeat. Jim Callaghan belonged to the generation of Labour leaders which had come to depend on the trade union block vote for protection against extremism in the constituencies; moreover, the trade unions had provided his main political base in the previous decade.

That base was now crumbling. Again and again in the critical years after the 1979 election, incoherence or incompetence in the trade union leadership led us to disaster.

Denis Healey, *The Time of My Life*, Harmondsworth, 1990, pp. 467–8.

5.2 Whom to blame?

> By no means all members accepted the leadership's analysis. In the weeks following the 1979 election, *Tribune* invited contributions to a 'Great Debate' on the cause of defeat. Many correspondents considered that government policy had led the electorate to support the Conservatives. The need for more 'socialism' was, from this point of view, paramount. Here Alan Taylor, Labour's unsuccessful candidate for Weston-super-Mare, makes his view of the matter plain enough.

I do not think that Labour's defeat in the general election is fundamentally important. We have had a conservative monetarist Government since 1976. The electorate has now rejected a party which pursued such policies without liking them and chosen a party which openly embraces them.

These policies were adopted in 1976 because public opinion had gone that way. The International Monetary Fund coup merely confirmed this choice. It is now our task to win back public opinion to a socialist view, so that we can force the Conservatives on the defensive, and eventually elect a Labour Government which can implement socialist policies since they are actively backed by the electorate.

The 'winter of discontent' did not cause our defeat. I think we would have lost last October, and next October too. The reason is that we lacked credibility as a conservative monetarist Government. Our Government looked tired, old, and unconvincing. The winter's strikes merely exaggerated this impression.

A Labour Government following such policies alienates many of its supporters without winning over its opponents.... I found doorstep comment in this election remarkably ideological. People were really talking about the Tory line on incentives as a way of revitalising the economy. With a genuine experience of bureaucracy failing to deliver the goods, of taxes and public spending which often failed to produce value for money, and of continuing industrial decline, people were won over by the Conservative message of incentives, tax cuts, and less government.

Tribune, 18 May 1979.

5.3 The need for accountability

According to left-wing analysis, Labour lost in 1979 because the leadership had ignored policies adopted by conference whilst the Party was in opposition during 1970–73. Only by reflecting its members' wishes would Labour's fortunes revive. This was the opinion of the Campaign for Labour Party Democracy, which since 1973 had attempted to increase the accountability of the PLP.

The first priority for the Party to face is what the Tory victory means. The gentlemanly Jim Callaghan, when congratulating Mrs Thatcher, spoke of 'that great office ... wonderful privilege' and 'tremendous moment in the country's history' as a woman becomes Prime Minister. It was certainly no 'tremendous moment' for the Labour Party. 'That great office' will enable Mrs Thatcher to preside over a major re-distribution of income from working people to a small minority of the wealthy.

The second priority for the Party to face, and a harder one, is a completely honest analysis of the causes of the election debacle. It might start with the rejection of the idea that Labour lost the election because voters preferred the Tory promises. If elections were won on the relative merits of election manifestos, then even the Labour Party's emasculated effort would have won hands down over the Tory mixture of demagoguery and empty bribes. What must be recognised is that governments lose elections because of their record.

The last Labour government came to power on the hopes of working people that it would protect their interests; instead they were confronted with unjust wage norms, public spending cuts and high unemployment. Alternative policies advocated by Labour Party conference and the TUC were never seriously considered. It is because of the Labour government's policies that the Labour Party was unable to mobilise its electoral strength. It is these policies that caused Labour's potential supporters to switch to Mrs Thatcher.

No doubt Labour's parliamentary leadership will waste little time in trying to place the blame for the defeat on the trade unionists' lack of discipline and on alleged left-wing infiltrators. It would be idle to pretend that the events of the last winter did not alienate some Labour supporters. But those who took part in industrial action – above all the low paid – were driven to this by the Labour government's wages policy which demanded a far greater sacrifice from them than from the better off.

... The parliamentary leadership of the Party has repeatedly shown its inability to learn from its mistakes as well as its unwillingness to promote policies based on Labour Party conference decisions. If the Party is to retain credibility with those who it is representing, its Leader and MPs must be made more accountable. This alone will provide the necessary safeguard to enable the implementation of Labour Party policies.

Campaign for Labour Party Democracy Newsletter, May–June 1979, p. 1.

5.4   A member wants a voice

The call for more accountability was associated, in the eyes of contemporary political commentators, with entryists and ex-student radicals. This ignored the fact that activists, such as those in Victory For Socialism, had long called for reform. Here, a sixty-one-year-old widow described as 'comfortably off' and a member of Putney CLP since the late 1950s describes her view of the matter. She hardly conforms to the stereotype of a bedsit militant.

I think it is justifiable and inevitable that those people who do most of the work in the party should have the greatest influence in forming policy. No one would agree to do the drudgery if they did not have the chance of occasionally making their point of view felt. The changes under discussion, more influence for party members, are at present the subject of adverse comments in the press. It is said that a tiny minority wants to run the party; but these are people who do the work. It's not an exclusive club and in my opinion it is quite justified in any organisation that the voices of those who work in it shall be heard more than those who are only passengers; indeed, it is almost inevitable. There are many members of the Labour Party, and for ten years I was one of them, who just pay their subs and do nothing else at all. These people should not be despised if that is all they can manage but those who go to meetings must have more influence in forming policy and they are entitled to that influence.

Hugh Jenkins, *Rank and File*, London, 1980, pp. 35–6

5.5   The local dimension

The call for more democracy was not only due to the leadership's performance in office. By the late 1970s activists refused to tolerate the way numerous CLPs, particularly in safe constituencies, were run. Peter Tatchell was candidate in the 1983 Bermondsey by-election, which saw that solid, 'traditional' working-class, Labour constituency fall to the Liberals. Here he describes the situation in the constituency. Between 1946 and 1983 Bermondsey was represented by Bob Mellish,[1] who, by the time he resigned, viewed his local party activists with contempt. In the by-election he even refused to endorse Tatchell, and supported a 'Real Labour Party' candidate.

The constituency party held little or no political debate. It seemed to exist to re-elect local worthies to Southwark council (which covers the Bermondsey area) and to re-elect Mellish to Parliament. The party talked a lot about dustbins and memorial funds to retiring party workers, but very little else. Contact with the local community was practically nil. The General Committee

(GC), which is the decision-making body of the constituency party, never challenged the policies of the Labour-controlled Southwark council. The council was a gerontocracy, the average age of councillors being well over 60. One was nearly 90 and virtually immobile. Some had sat on the council continuously for over forty years. Undoubtedly, years ago some of them had given great service to the party. But now they were collectively so incompetent that in the 1978 borough council elections, the Labour manifesto was not issued until three weeks after the election! The party's attitude to Bob 'I'm the son of an 1889 docker' Mellish was deferential. Mellish ran Bermondsey as his personal fiefdom and brooked no opposition; not that there was much in the flaccid ranks of the right wing.... The whole party revolved around Mellish, Goodwin, O'Grady and the councillors. Like a dynasty, this handful of ruling families, often related by marriage, used their positions to perpetuate their rule and sit on any burgeoning opposition.

... The members wanted to participate in a meaningful way in Labour party decision-making. They wanted their elected representatives to be accountable. They wanted to be consulted by councillors about council policy. They did not want to carry on being treated as donkeys on whose backs the councillors and the MP were elected. The mood of unrest in Bermondsey was duplicated in many constituencies elsewhere. It helped to bring about the major changes in the party's constitution at the 1980 annual conference. The party rank and file were in effect saying, the Labour Party belongs to its membership, not to its leaders or its elected representatives.

Peter Tatchell, *The Battle for Bermondsey*, London, 1983, pp. 16, 35.

5.6 The promise of success

The left was optimistic that a genuinely 'socialist' Party would generate more support amongst the electorate than hitherto. In this excerpt from a contemporary pamphlet, Peter Hain, a leading member of the then left-leaning Labour Coordinating Committee and later an MP, lists seven reasons for being cheerful. The result of the 1983 general election suggests that his analysis was ill-founded.

First, we have had since May 3 1979 a right-wing rather than a social democratic government in office, heralding an end to the post-War consensus politics that have been practised whatever Party was in power.... Radical socialism is now on the agenda ... because of the Conservatives' own break with middle way politics and their lurch into right-wing monetarism.

Second, the Tories' policies are exacerbating the more general economic recession and crisis of capitalism, and will increasingly provoke opposition from workers regardless of what the Labour Party does. Thatcherism is specifically designed to attack working class living standards and to undermine working class power. As resistance on wages, jobs and cuts grows, so the opportunity for a political input to struggles that would otherwise remain 'economistic' will grow....

The *third* advantageous factor is that a political vacuum has opened up within the trade union movement at the key level of rank-and-file activists. The shop stewards movement is much weaker now than in the 1960s and early 1970s.... Workplace activists are crying out for a radical socialist lead....

Fourthly, there is a growing feeling amongst many of a progressive or radical persuasion who busied themselves in 'single-issue' politics in the 1960s and 1970s that a broader political movement is necessary....

Fifth, the growth of the women's movement has opened up a vital extra dimension to socialist politics and enabled women to get involved in political action on *their* terms, pushing specifically women's issues onto the political agenda....

Sixth, the far left is emphatically not enjoying the expansion that might have been anticipated in the aftermath of the Wilson/Callaghan regimes and under the threat of Thatcherism. Indeed the organised left outside the Labour Party is in crisis.

Seventh, youth politics – which in the late 1960s especially developed its own distinctive momentum – is now in disarray. The alternatives to the Labour Party look far less attractive than they did in the days of hippies and the student revolt.

Peter Hain, *On Reviving the Labour Party*, Nottingham, not dated, pp. 2–3.

5.7 Labour's new constituency

Inner-city activists – most prominently in London – saw little merit in appealing to skilled workers, most of whom had moved to places such as Essex. Instead, they wanted to create a coalition of the dispossessed, amongst whom were women, blacks, gays and the very poor. This strategy contrasted with the national leadership's desire to win back 'affluent' workers, many of whom had voted Conservative in 1979. In an interview Ken Livingstone, then leader of the Labour-controlled Greater London Council and a future MP, outlined his vision.

... we have to start to articulate the needs of the minorities and the dispossessed in a way that Labour governments and the Labour Party never have in the past. I mean the *very* poor have never done well out of a Labour government. They've usually lost out quite considerably. They tended to be neglected. And that has to be a change we make within the Labour Party – the minorities have to be represented, the lower income groups have to be represented, and we have to look to their interests as well as the interests of the organised working class in skilled trade unions.

Now how you reach these people isn't easy to see. I mean a lot of them can be reached by approaching them on an issue basis rather than a simple class approach. For a lot of them what matters, particularly the younger element in London, is our position on an issue. The issue of women, or the issue of blacks or the issue of gays or whatever....

I think there could be setbacks, we could be defeated. But our real problem to overcome is that a lot of these groups look on the Labour Party with a record of 30 years of betrayal and defeat. *We* actually have got to establish first that we're different from what's gone before, that we are not prepared to back down and make all sorts of immediate compromises necessary to save our jobs.

Marxism Today, November 1981.

5.8 Hostility to Party 'democracy'

Within the PLP even those on the 'old' left were critical of most of the constitutional reforms passed by conference after 1979. They resented Tony Benn's influence and saw his support for accountability as motivated by personal ambition. They also made a more serious case for the MP to be seen as a 'representative' rather than a 'delegate'. Peter Shore[2] made this case in a speech delivered during the summer of 1981 at the height of Benn's deputy leadership campaign.

A month ago, I said that what Mr Benn was about was the creation of a New Model Party. A Party to be created not out of new policies – for the differences here are certainly reconcilable – but out of a radical new doctrine and practice for party democracy.

Mr Benn, like the Calvinists of the 16th Century, believes that Labour Members and supporters are divided into the Elect and non-Elect – and that he uniquely represents the former. The Party Elect are not the activists, the men and women who do the hard work of the Party in the constituencies. The Elect are the Elect, not because of their work but because of their faith and their ideology. They are not even necessarily socialists – although some are of an unusual kind. But they certainly are zealots. And it is the principal characteristic of zealots throughout the ages that they are intolerant, fanatical and authoritarian. They are, in Benn's New Model Army, the Ironsides, drilled and trained, anxious and ready for war: for civil war. And if they win, they will be just as ready to execute the elected monarch as to crush the Levellers.

It is because they believe they are the Elect that the normal rules of Party conduct and democracy do not apply. Against decisions – whether they be those of Annual Conference, the Manifesto, the Parliamentary Party or the Shadow Cabinet – of which they disapprove, they claim the right, the total freedom, even the duty, to challenge and to flaunt. For decisions which they do support, they demand instant obedience and the suppression of all further debate. When they are in the ascendant, majority rule, democratic centralism, becomes a sacred duty. When they are in the minority, the right to argue, to dissent, to protest and disobey become the very lifeblood of democracy.

There is, according to their lights, nothing inconsistent in these attitudes. Since they are the Elect, they must in both cases be right....

I have always believed that MP's should be accountable to their parties and that parties have the right to remove MP's who either are not serving their constituency interests or with whom, seriously and honestly, on a range of issues they cannot agree. And it is the pride of MP's that they should be able to win and to hold the understanding and support of their local parties and their constituents. That is democratic accountability.

But this is not the same as the new coercive accountability that is now being demanded and introduced; the accountability of loyal oaths, the accountability of individual ratings and score sheets on carefully selected test issues.

This is vital. For there is indeed a fundamental difference between the MP and the local councillor as a representative, guided by the convictions he shares with his Party, anxious in all the debates and discussions that he will encounter in the forums of democracy to carry out the policies and to realise the ends that they both share; and the MP, as a mandated delegate, carrying out the instructions of his GMC. As Michael Foot said, the Party deserves something better than 'honourable midgets and the Rt. Hon. marionettes', performing in 'a castrated House of Commons'.

LPA, Michael Foot papers, MF/Box L4/File: 'Tony Benn and the Deputy Leadership 1981', transcript of a speech delivered by Peter Shore to a meeting of Labour Solidarity in Cardiff, 5 June 1981, pp. 4, 8.

5.9   Social democrats and the politics of collectivism

In contrast to the left's opinion that increased state control would attract more voters, Labour's increasingly discontented social democrats thought that a greater role for the state would be electorally disastrous. Their view was that the majority now opposed more government. Here Shirley Williams,[3] soon to found the SDP, outlines such a view.

The political mood in the West has changed remarkably in recent years. The balance of opinion has moved against the typical product of social democratic government: government intervention in the economy, high public sector expenditure, the welfare state, a substantial public sector and the pursuit of equality. The intellectual winds now blow from a different quarter; the right-wing thinkers show more energy and confidence than do left-wing thinkers, many of whom reiterate tired and irrelevant dogmas or seem incapable of moving beyond their last stated position....

Many socialist policies have depended upon the state as their instrument; they have required an expansion in the role of central government. Socialists need to recognize the force of the antipathy that now exists towards 'big government': the multiplication of bureaucracy, the increase in cost, the feeling that government already has too large an influence over people's individual lives....

Socialists may dismiss public unease on this score, but they would be foolish to do so. For the resentment towards big government and its public expression, bureaucracy, is not just a resentment inspired by inefficiency. It goes much deeper than that.... It is a powerful desire to run oneself and one's own show, not to be bothered with forms and regulations, not to be treated, however rationally, as a unit rather than as a person.

Shirley Williams, *Politics is for People*, Harmondsworth, 1981, pp. 28–9.

5.10 Reasons for leaving Labour

Those who resigned from Labour to establish the SDP in 1981 often complained that the Party had fundamentally changed since the 1960s. According to them, Labour had become undemocratic and unrepresentative. Here, William Rodgers puts the general case for leaving the Party. Whilst those such as Denis Healey and Roy Hattersley might have agreed with much of his analysis, they decided to remain and fight.

The internal developments in the Labour Party in the eighteen months following its defeat of May 1979 determined the manner and timing of the break [to form the SDP] but they were not its root cause. These developments were a symptom of the same flight from reality which had prevented the Labour Party seeing its position plainly over many years.... Throughout the 1960s and 1970s, no serious attempt was made by the leadership of the Labour Party to ensure its relevance to the problems that Britain faced in the remaining years of the century. This failure created the opportunities for those who cared little for the Labour Party's tradition of tolerance and commitment to Parliamentary democracy, or, alternatively, chose to pursue policies remote from the facts of political life....

In the past, the trade unions had provided the balancing mechanism in a clumsy but deliberate fashion. They had recognized the importance of a large measure of independence for Members of Parliament and a major role for the Parliamentary Labour Party in the complex organism their forebears had helped to create.... Now their leaders either failed to grasp or chose to acquiesce in the steady erosion of long-standing relationships between sections of the party....

The trade union leaders were accustomed to share in policy-making and to state their interests to the Parliamentary leadership of the Party. But they had generally recognized the wider obligations the Party assumed when in power, both at Westminster and in local government. Now they were unwilling or unable to restrain those of their members who sought to establish direct control over decisions affecting their terms and conditions of employment. In the public service unions, young, graduate organizers with no attachment to the democratic Left saw opportunities for hiring-and-firing their own employers, especially when they were local Councillors. Little attempt was made to discover whether they acted on behalf of their members or to assess the extent to which they were alienating support from the Labour Party. The trade union leadership had abrogated its responsibility to lead.

William Rodgers, *The Politics of Change*, London, 1982, pp. 167–8.

5.11 Benn's deputy leadership campaign

The zenith of the left's influence occurred during Tony Benn's attempt to become deputy leader in 1981. He wished to replace the much-hated Healey. Such a move revealed cracks in the alliance which had helped pass many internal reforms at conference. Thus, MPs like Neil Kinnock refused to support a campaign which they saw as electorally damaging. A number of trade union leaders also questioned Benn's move for similar reasons. In this account, Michael Foot, leader during this difficult time, describes his view of the contest.

1981 could and should have been the year in which the Labour movement applied all its energies to concert united vengeance for the wounds inflicted upon our people and to destroy the Tory Government. Instead, we turned it into a period of futility and shame, and the responsibility for transmuting every controversy of the time into an internal Labour Party dispute rested directly with Tony Benn. One of the first steps which the National Executive took at the beginning of the year, with my full support, was to organise a series of demonstrations against the most obvious scourge and the source of almost every other social ill, the rising flood of mass unemployment.... The lead was given, and every section of the movement showed its eagerness to respond. The first great demonstration was staged at Liverpool, and it was a mammoth and unmitigated success: it showed what could be done by unity in the right cause. The second demonstration was at Cardiff, and was well-nigh wrecked by a sectarian mob (mostly imported from outside Wales) on the side, screaming applause for Tony Benn and execrations on Denis Healey. The third in Birmingham was wrecked absolutely by even wilder and more indiscriminate scenes of sectarian shrieking....

All other political events within the Labour Party for the scavenger Tory press and the vulturous television cameras had been overtaken by the decision of Tony Benn to challenge Denis Healey for the deputy-leadership of the Party under the new electoral college system. He had embarked upon the contest despite pleadings from every quarter, mine almost to the foremost.... And truly, no skill in prediction was needed to see what would happen. The Cardiff and Birmingham fiascos were only the most spectacular. A whole hot, ugly summer followed. Week by week, the areas of dispute were enlarged, the gulf cut deeper, while our Tory opponents watched in gleeful disbelief and gratitude....

This deputy-leadership election was surely no 'healing process', as he described it. He was out to win, whatever happened, and as we came nearer to the end, he and his closest backers thought they were winning, right up to the Saturday night of 27 September, before the result was declared. Throughout the day, at the pre-Conference meeting of the Executive, he used his majority there to push through one proposition after another he favoured, often overturning the advice of the Party officials who warned against the folly of accepting commitments which had never been costed. Nothing else counted. He thought the next day would mark the climax of all his exertions of those years. Not the absolute climax, of course; that would come when he would be able to stand and win the next full leadership fight – no doubt after yet another 'healing process'.

Michael Foot, *Loyalists and Loners*, London, 1986, pp. 122–4.

5.12   The Party still divided

The minutes of the Eccleshill ward branch of the Bradford North CLP reveal that not all members agreed with Foot's assessment of the Benn campaign. This is not surprising as Bradford was one of a number of places in which the Militant Tendency was active. Militant influence was contested: in this discussion of the 1981 conference the respective positions are revealed.

Mr Dyson ... said that the Conference seemed to emit a mood towards the original socialist ideas of the Party. He said that this was the most reactionary Government since the war, which seemed determined to smash the Labour Party and Trade Unions through its policies.

He felt that the previous Labour Party Government's policies were not enough, they had failed successively. The policies discussed at this year's conference were more in line with socialist principles. He felt that the failure of Mr Benn to secure the Deputy Leadership was not a defeat, but merely a setback caused by the abstention of certain M.P.s.

He also felt that the Trade Unions should have honoured their members in block votes where certain T.U. leaders had voted against their members' wishes....

He said that there was an overwhelming mood towards a unified move towards socialist policies, and an apparent determination to carry through those policies.... He thought that those policies would result in a clear majority for the Labour Party at the next General Election....

Mr Midwood stated that until a 'broad church' of the Labour Party is seen by the general public, they will not be happy with the Party, and that there is too much intolerance between members.

Mr Hare stated that he thought there was a definite move towards socialism, where everyone should tolerate everyone else's point of view. He said that the Labour Party has, in the past, been a Party of bureaucrats, but that changes were needed, and that tolerance works both ways....

Mr Dyson, in summing up, said that the Party and Trade Unions would only gain credibility through democracy, but also suggested that there should be no witchhunts or proscribed lists.

LPA, Michael Foot papers, MF/Box L4/File: 'Correspondence re: reselection and the left, 1981–83', minutes of Eccleshill branch Labour Party, 3 November 1981.

Permanent opposition? 1983–92

Labour not only failed to win the 1983 general election, it also nearly fell to third place in terms of the popular vote, behind the SDP and Liberal alliance. The Party's divisions since 1979 and an unpopular manifesto made the centre parties attractive to many accustomed Labour voters. Various commentators predicted that Labour was fated to become the party of the ever-diminishing and increasingly pauperised 'traditional' working class. This was Michael Foot's legacy to Neil Kinnock. Straight after becoming leader in the autumn of 1983, Kinnock emphasised the need for Labour to reconnect with the concerns of most voters. To this end, he set about marginalising Tony Benn and his supporters. This was a tortuous process: by the 1987 general election Labour policy had changed little in substance – nor did the Party's vote increase by much. After this third successive defeat Kinnock's 'modernisation' of the Party accelerated. Whilst he presented change as the only way for Labour to regain power, critics accused Kinnock of emulating SDP and even Conservative policies. By the 1992 general election Labour had discarded most of the policies on offer in 1983; it was still rejected at the polls. Had the Kinnock years been a waste of time?

6.1   A victory for 'socialism'

Tony Benn was one of many Labour MPs to lose their seats in 1983. This was generally considered a disaster, but Benn saw merit in the result. Rather than viewing the election as the Party's post-war nadir, to Benn it appeared a solid base on which to build support. There was, he concluded, no need to change the programme presented to the British people in 1983.

The General Election of 1983 has produced one important result that has passed virtually without comment in the media. It is that, for the first time since 1945, a political party with an openly socialist policy has received the support of over 8½ million people. This is a remarkable development by any standards and it deserves some analysis.

... the 1983 Labour manifesto commanded the loyalty of millions of voters and a democratic socialist bridge-head has been established from which further advances in public understanding and support can be made.

This largely unreported event will I believe have far more relevance to the future of our society than the highly marginal differences of emphasis that exist between the SDP/Liberal MPs, some of them elected on tactical votes, and the Tory Government.

Inevitably it will be those very peripheral and personalised encounters which will now be presented by lobby correspondents as if they constituted the only real choice that is now before the nation. Yet behind this diversionary noise will lie the mounting despair of the unemployed, the young, the old, the sick and disabled and the low paid, women as well as men, black as well as white.

If any of these people are allowed the chance to hear them they will find a great deal of encouragement from the arguments coming from the Labour Party as it rediscovers its Socialism after so many years.

Guardian, 20 June 1983.

6.2   The need to get in touch with 'reality'

> In contrast to Benn, Kinnock thought 1983 demonstrated the extent to which the Party had lost touch with the voters. In formally accepting the post of leader at the conference which followed defeat, Kinnock set out his perspective. By invoking the words of Aneurin Bevan, Kinnock hoped to reassure delegates that he remained a man of the left – if by no means a Bennite.

Here in this crowded, dangerous, beautiful world, there is only hope if there is hope together for all peoples. Our function, our mission, our objective as socialists is to see that we gain the power to achieve that....

To get that we have to win, and we must be of the people, and for the people. If we want guidance in how to win, we look no further than the man you would expect me to quote on this day of all days, Aneurin Bevan, my fellow countryman, my fellow townsman, my inspiration. (*Applause*)

Nye said, as a maxim for a political leader, and I commend it as a maxim for a political movement:

He who would lead must articulate the wants, the frustrations and the aspirations of the majority. Their hearts must be moved, so his words must be attuned to their realities. If he speaks in the old false categories, they will listen and at first nod their heads, for they hear a familiar echo from the past; but if he persists, they begin to appreciate that he is no longer with them. He must speak with the authentic accents of those who elected him. That means that he should share their values, that he is in touch with their realities.

... That is how we win. If anyone wants to know why we must conduct ourselves in this fashion, just remember at all times ... how you, each and every one of you, sitting in this hall, each and every Labour worker watching this conference, each and every Labour voter, yes, and some others as well, remember how you felt on that dreadful morning of 10 June. Just remember how you felt then, and think to yourselves: 'June the Ninth, 1983; never ever again will we experience that'. (*Applause*)

Report of the Annual Conference of the Labour Party, 1983, London, 1983, p. 30.

6.3 The difficulty of reforming the Party

In order to get the Party back in touch with 'reality', Kinnock sought to change policy. In so doing, he was convinced of the need to destroy the position of what was by now described as the 'hard' left. In this account, delivered after his resignation as leader, Kinnock revealed the basis of his strategy.

Even before the General Election of 1983, and as I began to campaign for election as Leader, it was clear to me and to those associated with me that there would have to be profound changes in the policies and in the organisation of the Labour Party – not simply as ends in themselves but also as contributions to the change in the mentality of the Labour Party.

Some around me at the time hoped that the lessons of defeat would be so convincing that they would automatically produce a mandate for radical change, especially with a Leader who had secured 71 per cent of the vote in the Leadership contest. I did not share that optimism. It was plain to me that the majority of affiliated trade unions had policies and leaderships that would be difficult to shift to different stances. It was also evident that the majority of Constituency Labour Parties – or, at least, the people who led them and spoke for those parties – would be resistant to substantial or speedy changes in most of the existing policies of the Labour Party in 1983.

... in the Labour Party, the leadership had no instrument for inaugurating and pursuing change on the scale and in the direction that was needed. There was no tradition of the PLP or the Shadow Cabinet instituting and processing comprehensive change and neither was there any means available for doing that. The National Executive Committee was still, in 1983, a body with a slight majority against the Leadership on most issues which involved alteration in the policy and constitutional position of the party.

It is a sad fact of life that, in the absence of any mechanism for instigating change, even the strongest and most dedicated Leadership will-power is not an adequate engine of reform. And that difficulty is, of course, particularly pronounced in the Labour Party where the authority over the Constitution is vested in the Conference, where the NEC is elected annually and matches the federal nature of the party and, unlike the Conservative Party, the Shadow Cabinet is not within the gift of the Leader's appointment.

In referring to those features, I am neither advocating change in those institutional arrangements nor am I offering excuses. My purpose is simply to identify realities which have to be coped with by any leader who – by necessity or by preference – adds managerial responsibility and reforming determination to his or her general political duties to the party.

In my case, of course, the managerial role was a matter of necessity ... the condition of the party made management an obligation – so I got on with it.

Neil Kinnock, 'Reforming the Labour Party', *Contemporary Record*, 8:3, 1994, pp. 536–7.

6.4 Kinnock defines his 'socialism'

For his pains, Kinnock was criticised by those on the 'hard' left for being an unprincipled pragmatist rather than a 'socialist'. They accused him of turning his back on his former beliefs. Kinnock was sensitive to this charge and, in his own mind, remained a 'socialist', and continued to claim direct lineage from Bevan. As this summary of his beliefs makes plain, it was a 'socialism' defined by the need to achieve equality, democracy and liberty. Largely owing to continued Conservative success, Kinnock's stress on the last aspect became ever-more pronounced as the decade advanced.

[The] object past, present and future of democratic socialism [is] individual freedom. And the means which democratic socialism has chosen to protect that freedom are equality and democracy. Just as freedom unqualified by law leaves the weak unprotected from violence, so freedom unqualified by democracy and equality leaves the weak unprotected from power. That is why the values of liberty, equality and democracy are interdependent to democratic socialism. And it is that belief in their *interdependence* which makes the analysis, the code of beliefs and the criteria for success employed by democratic socialism different from the approach taken by other ideologies which may, with sincerity, believe in liberty and equality or democracy as single purposes.

The liberty of individuals and of societies is an absolute value to democratic socialists. But, too often, socialism has been associated with the very opposite – parodied by its association with an uncaring bureaucracy. At times we seem to have permitted a set of beliefs that begins from this practical desire to foster the political and economic liberty of all people to look like a dogma that regarded liberty as a tedious bourgeois fad.

... We need to convey ... that there is no essential contradiction between collective provision and individual freedom since the one reinforces and makes possible the other. As socialists the advancement of collective freedoms is central precisely because it offers the best hope of advancing individual freedom.

It is essential to reassert that primary value at a time when every malaise from commercial failure to crime is blamed upon the mythical 'degeneracy' which allegedly resulted from thirty or so years of feather-bedding, family splitting welfare state provision....

Collective provision has not been the enemy of individual freedom, it has been the agent of individual emancipation and for that reason it will occupy a central position in the forging of the future of socialism.

Neil Kinnock, *The Future of Socialism*, Fabian tract number 509, London, 1985, pp. 3–5.

6.5   Kinnock's 'Militant' speech

The year 1984–85 presented Kinnock with numerous difficulties. It was the 'lost year' in which the miners' strike took precedence over moving Labour towards 'reality'. The 1985 conference was dominated by accusations of betrayal from those who blamed the miners' defeat on Kinnock's reluctance to give them his unqualified support. This conference was also the occasion for one of his most famous speeches, in which he referred to the activities of the Militant-led Labour Liverpool City Council. As this transcript indicates, not all Kinnock's audience appreciated his views.

There are some in our movement who ... accuse me of an obsession with electoral politics; there are some who, when I say we must reach out and make a broader appeal to those who only have their labour to sell, who are part of the working classes – no doubt about their credentials – say that I am too preoccupied with winning; there are some who say, when I reach out like that and in the course of seeking out that objective, that I am prepared to compromise values. I say to them and I say to everybody else, and I mean it from the depths of my soul: there is no need to compromise values, there is no need in this task to surrender our socialism, there is no need to abandon or even try to hide any of our principles, but there is an implacable need to win and there is an equal need for us to understand that we address an electorate which is sceptical, an electorate which needs convincing, a British public who want to know that our idealism is not lunacy, our realism is not timidity, our eagerness is not extremism, a British public who want to know that our carefulness too is not nervousness.

... Because you are from the people, because you are of the people, because you live with the same realities as everybody else lives with, implausible promises don't win victories. I'll tell you what happens with impossible promises. You start with far-fetched resolutions. They are then pickled into a rigid dogma, a code and you go through the years sticking to that, out-dated, misplaced, irrelevant to the real needs, and you end up in the grotesque chaos of a Labour council hiring taxis to scuttle round a city handing out redundancy notices to its own workers. (*Applause*) I am telling you, no matter how entertaining, how fulfilling to short-term egos – (*Continuing applause*) – you can't play politics with people's jobs and with people's services or with their homes. (*Applause and some boos*) Comrades, the voice of the people – not the people here; the voice of the real people with real needs – is louder than all the boos that can be assembled. Understand that, please, comrades. In your socialism, in your commitment to those people, understand it. The people will not, cannot, abide posturing. They cannot respect the gesture-generals or the tendency-tacticians.

Report of the Annual Conference of the Labour Party, 1985, London, 1985, pp. 127, 128.

6.6   The 'Militant' speech refuted

Kinnock's approach to Militant was not universally welcomed. To mark his protest, Eric Heffer, Liverpool MP and long-time NEC member, walked off the platform whilst Kinnock concluded his attack on Liverpool Council. Heffer was a critic of the Party's move from its 1983 programme. In his posthumously published autobiography he gave his opinion of Kinnock's performance.

131

Neil Kinnock did something most unusual at Conference and decided to wind up for the NEC on the miners.... Neil Kinnock's hostility to the miners' leaders was shown not so much in what he said, although at times that was bad enough, but in the tone he used. His face set hard and he spat out his words. He was to adopt the same demeanour when he came to discuss the situation in Liverpool where the council was facing a devastating cash crisis....

Kinnock proceeded to launch a vicious attack on the Liverpool council from the platform of the conference. He gave the impression that it was dominated and run by the Militant Tendency. Certainly Militants were on the council but they were a small minority. I knew that the council had built good houses – good houses; that it had built sports centres to keep the youth off the streets. It had kept council rents and the price of school dinners down. It had provided the elderly with telephones. It had effected long overdue reorganization of education and put a race relations officer in each school. It had created a new park and cleared slums which should have been cleared years before. It made tactical errors but those who try to do positive things sometimes make mistakes.

Kinnock's aim was to split the unity of the councillors and the party in the city.... It was too much to bear. I walked off the platform while Kinnock was still speaking, only to hear him say, after the uproar, 'You can't play politics with people's jobs.' He *knew* the council was not doing that.

... Kinnock has proved to be a great cynical manipulator who has used the party's dislike and fear of Thatcher to get revisionist policies accepted. He has gone farther than Gaitskell in revising the party's principles, policies and organization. He has got away with it because the party elected him in the belief that he was a left-wing leader who would carry out socialist policies. What an illusion that turned out to be.

Eric Heffer, *Never A Yes Man. The Life and Politics of an Adopted Liverpudlian*, London, pp. 212–13, 230.

6.7 Making Labour 'acceptable'

Gavin Laird, general secretary of the Amalgamated Engineering Union (AEU), was interviewed in the *New Statesman* in the wake of the 1987 general election. His union had one of the most powerful voices at the Labour conference. The AEU's members were also largely affluent, skilled manual workers – the sort who had increasingly abandoned Labour since the 1970s and whose support the Party needed in the late 1980s.

I've just been at the annual meeting of the Confederation of Shipbuilding and Engineering Unions and I heard a whole series of speeches that I heard ten years ago. Nothing has changed as far as they're concerned. So what I tried to say is that we've fallen victim to our own propaganda: the reality is that, whereas there is all too big a section of underprivileged people in the country, real standards for the rest have improved substantially....

What was very encouraging to me was the recognition a couple of years ago that the Labour Party's traditional stance on housing had to change, and change it did. But there appears to be a marked reluctance in other areas. What's wrong with people wanting cars? What's wrong with people wanting their own house? If in the States you speak to a guy who assembles cars, he sees no difference between himself and a doctor or a lawyer except in earning power. There's none of this class differentiation. It seems to me that we're heading in the same direction, and what's wrong with that? We should recognise that and tailor the party's programme to it. That's not opportunism, that's recognising people's aspirations.

That then presents problems for the party because you've got to look at how you formulate your programme. To take our union, we've always prided ourselves on our democracy, and yet for all that the policy body that determines what we will do for the next 12 months is 124 people, excellent people, activists, but are they terribly representative? Because they come from our branches and less than 2 per cent of our members attend the branches. And so the trade unions and the Labour Party reflect a very narrow part of our own movement....

We're that damned anxious to reflect our members' views, but we're not doing very well when it comes to those that vote Tory. But it would stick in my craw to have to advocate policies that are not pro-Labour policies. So what am I about? I'm about trying to ensure that the policies the Labour Party pursues are acceptable to the broad mass of our members. We canna' be 16 steps ahead of our members all the time.

New Statesman, 10 July 1987.

6.8   There is no 'rainbow coalition'

After the 1987 defeat the 'soft' left increasingly distanced itself from the 'hard' left and gave Kinnock's reforms qualified support. Michael Meacher[1] was a former Benn confidant: his personal trajectory reflected a more general shift from old positions. In this excerpt Meacher accepts that Labour could not rely on the 'traditional' working class or a 'rainbow coalition' of the dispossessed as he had once hoped.

It is the technocratic class – the semi-conductor 'chip' designers, the computer operators, the industrial research scientists, the high-tech engineers – who hold the key to Britain's future. That is the class that Labour must champion and bring to power if it is to break out into the Midlands and South.

Labour must also find the means to convince the electorate that we can really deliver. The social policies [presented by Labour in the 1987 campaign] are wanted, but will a Labour Government be tough enough to take the hard-nosed decisions over public order, inflation and the economy to make these social aspirations viable? Given that Neil Kinnock represents probably the strongest Labour leader for decades, it should not prove an impossible task.

Critically, there is no Rainbow Coalition of minorities that will bring Labour back to power. Important though blacks, gays, the women's movement, the peace movement, and the unemployed are, they are not enough.

The growing underclass of have-nots, large and desperate though it is, can only in the end come to power through policies that assist, and are seen to assist, the not-so-poor and not-so-powerless. The welding together of these disparate groups into a single coherent, dominant political force becomes now Labour's prime task.

Guardian, 25 June 1987.

6.9   How to improve Labour's appeal

Bryan Gould[2] was Labour's campaign manager in the 1987 general election. Despite defeat, Labour's campaign was widely considered its most effective ever. Here, Gould assesses which direction Labour needed to take after 1987. Echoing the views of Laird and Meacher, he indicates that a change in strategy was required if Labour was to prosper. He also made plain his belief that a fundamental transformation of Party culture was necessary. This was, by now, a familiar – if usually unheeded – appeal.

We must of course make the Labour Party more open and accessible to a wider range of opinion and there is no reason why this should not include a greater willingness to listen to and talk to the Liberals – assuming that they have disowned the anti-Labour obsessions of the SDP. It may well be to our mutual advantage if we are seen to be on reasonably friendly terms, but the advantages to Labour of anything beyond that seem likely to be illusory.

So, in the absence of a short-cut, how do we improve our electoral appeal in our own right? The answer is partly a question of image, partly a question of organisation and partly a question of substantive policy. What is now required in each case is a consolidation and development of what has so far been achieved, rather than a renunciation of our recent history and sudden departure in substantially new directions.

We must first learn to give new and more welcoming signals to the electorate. This means being willing to talk in more modern language to those voters who have doubted our competence or trustworthiness in the past. We must reason rather than bluster. We must recognise their legitimate aims and aspirations rather than condemn them as class traitors. We must increasingly demonstrate our competence both in running our own affairs and in the critique we make in opposition to government policy.

This also has consequences for party organisation. If we are to present ourselves as a modern and democratic party, we must equip ourselves with the appropriate constitution and rules. This means that we must continue the process of democratisation and attract into membership a wider range of people. We must make it clear that the party is not the fiefdom of an activist elite, but is reaching out for support from, and welcomes the influence of, a wider range of opinion.

We must build on the renewed morale of the party and its supporters by offering more to those who are willing to join us. We should take a leaf out of the books of other voluntary organisations which, in return for membership subscription, do not simply demand further obligations – such as attending long and boring meetings – but actually provide something in return, in the form of information, publications, invitations to events and so on.

These outward-looking attitudes must also have their impact on policy-making. This does not mean that we have to move our policy to some hypothetical centrist position. The programme on which we fought the 1987 General Election was both radical and potentially attractive, and it is those qualities which now have to be strengthened. This is not just a matter of presentation; we have to sharpen up the process of policy formulation. We must ensure that we are not lumbered with policies which commend themselves to committees, but which cannot be sold to the electorate.

New Socialist, summer 1987.

6.10 The state of the 'hard' left in 1987

Tony Benn had lost much ground within the Party since 1983. By simply rejecting Kinnock's case that Labour had to change, Benn's support declined: it seemed to make no sense to ignore the electorate's verdict. The same was the case for those members of the Campaign Group who, like Benn, also saw little need to adapt policies which had won acceptance in the Party during the early 1980s. This is Benn's view of the state of the Party during the 1987 conference.

[26 September] In the evening we went to the Dome Theatre for the Campaign Group rally. It was a disaster, because the hall would have held 2000 and there were only 200, so it looked desolate. We are very much in the margins now; it isn't just the leadership that is running away, there is a total lack of confidence among the Party members.... These are very thin years for the left, but you have to think ahead.

[27 September] The arguments used by the leadership at today's pre-Conference NEC were more right-wing than I can remember for years. Geoff Bish[3] has swung to the right, recommending us against accepting any development of Party policy in a progressive direction....

I think the truth is that the Labour Party isn't believed any more because people suspect it will say anything to get votes. The rebuilding of some radical alternative to Thatcherism – and by that I mean all-party Thatcherism – will require us to do some very difficult things.

[2 October] My thoughts on leaving the Conference are that the whole thing was a media show. Socialism was mentioned in every sentence, and then by nudges and winks from the platform the media were told, 'Don't worry, we don't mean what we appear to mean.' They were using that to imply that the left were a ridiculous tiny majority against a socialist majority led by Kinnock.

There was a clear denial of class in everything that was said. What the Labour Party has done is to accept the Tory description of class – that there are the employed affluent workers on the one hand and the unemployed no-goods on the other – and to say the latter are an 'underclass' which just has to be catered for in some way.

Actually, the class distinction is between the very, very rich who live on dividends and who can afford to buy their house from their dividends, can afford to pay for their children's education, can afford to pay the full cost of medical care and can afford pensions from their own resources – all without working. But the docker from Bermondsey to whom Kinnock referred, earning £500 a week, with a car and a 'small place' in Marbella and a colour television, would be lost completely if he lost his job. So we represent people who depend for their living upon what they earn, and that is a distinction which puts the rich in a minority and labour in a majority.

Tony Benn, *The End of an Era. Diaries, 1980–90*, edited by Ruth Winstone, London, 1994, pp. 519, 522–3.

6.11   The purpose of the Policy Review

In the wake of the 1987 election and the resulting sense that
Labour had to take full account of its continued unpopularity, Kinnock launched a Policy Review, which continued
into 1989. This Review was meant to make Labour more
electable and yet stay faithful to the Party's basic principles.
The Policy Review's final report set out the leadership's
approach to the 1990s.

Labour's Policy Review is about change – the changes which are
happening and will happen, the changes which *we* want to bring
about, in Britain, in the rest of Europe and throughout the world.
In looking to the changes of the 1990s, however, we also have to
recognise the plain fact of the changes which have taken place in
the 1980s. Like every incoming government, the new Labour
government will have to build on what it finds, not on what it
would like to find. We shall begin from the early 1990s, not from
the late 1970s....

There is no real choice about *whether* to change. But there is a
choice about *how* Britain changes. Change can come as an
uncontrolled tide that buffets individuals, communities and
countries that are not ready to cope with its flow. Change can be
imposed, its victims – the poor, the redundant, the homeless – left
behind or beneath. Or change can be prepared for, guided,
controlled, its costs and its benefits shared throughout the
community. The past shapes us, but we make the future. The only
alternative therefore is between doing everything possible to see
that our country is on top of events, or veering away from that
path, trying to evade change and becoming its casualties instead
of its beneficiaries. Labour will take the first course.

As we do that, we will also be restoring responsible social
values to government. For Mrs Thatcher and the present
government, of course, 'there is no such thing as society'. To them
obligations of the community are a burden on the self-sufficient
individual, the individual needing opportunity and care is a
burden on the community. The state in their hands is intrusive
and centralising where it should hold back, and passive and
neglectful where it should protect and enable. As a result, public
squalor worsens, public standards are undermined. The *quality* of

life, first for the individuals most directly affected and then for all who make up the community, is cheapened and diminished....

Labour's attitude is very different. We have, of course, been caricatured as the party that seeks to deny power and choice to the individual and gather all authority to the state. The reality has always been different. To us the state is an instrument, no more, no less: a means, not an end. Collective action has always been designed to create opportunities and advance the freedom of the individual and, cumulatively, of the whole community.

We are conscious of the fact, however, that even a state with those liberating purposes can still become subject to vested interest. Throughout this Policy Review, therefore, we develop the case for a democratic, decentralised form of government, involving people as directly as possible in the decisions which affect them, using the accountable power of the state to help create a society in which citizens have the means and the self-assurance to take responsibility for their own lives and to fulfil their obligations to others. There is a limit to what the modern state can and should do. But there is no limit to what it can enable people to do for themselves.

... We do not work for dependence on the state. We work for dependable quality *from* the state. We want levels of contribution and provision that maximise the self-reliance which flourishes on opportunity and security and nourish the sense of responsibility which is essential to life in the modern community.

Labour Party, *Meet the Challenge, Make the Change. A New Agenda for Britain*, London, 1989, pp. 5, 6, 8.

6.12 The individual, community and state

As Kinnock's trade and industry spokesperson and an increasingly influential figure, Gordon Brown[4] was interviewed by *Marxism Today*. There, Brown took the opportunity to underline some of the points made in the Policy Review. He also anticipated an early theme of Tony Blair's leadership: 'community'. This excerpt is taken from his answer to the question 'Where do you draw from and what have you rejected in Labour's traditions?'

I used to study the history of socialism and the distinguishing feature of democratic socialism in Britain, as opposed to crude, free-market ideology, is that we believe that if individuals are to achieve their full potential then the community must act as a community, to enable that potential to develop. I think people would now accept that the state has got to be both active and accountable in the way it ensures that individuals have access to health care, to education, to affordable housing, to childcare; particularly at points in the life-cycle where things are difficult for individuals and for families. It's also true of the economy, where I believe that for prosperity to be achieved, the government and industry must be involved in that process. It cannot be left to crude, free-market forces.

The theme that runs through all this is the idea of a public interest. That there is a public agenda, and that there is a public good. It's not that individuals must sacrifice their own prosperity for that of the community; but that the community, by acting as a community, can enhance both individual potential and the prosperity of the economy. That is the distinguishing feature. And that leads you to ask: what can government do? How is the power of government used? In what form is it used? It leads on to all sorts of questions about the role of the state as enabler; as partner; as financier; in some cases as owner; as sponsor; as catalyst – not necessarily a unilinear or a uniform role. And it also leads on to huge questions that we have not properly answered in the past, but are beginning to answer now: about the devolution of power; about decentralisation; about communities being able to manage their own affairs; about devolution particularly to regional levels and tiers of government.

Marxism Today, January 1991.

6.13   Taxation and the 1992 general election

Despite facing a weakened Conservative government, Labour nevertheless lost the 1992 general election. There were many possible causes of defeat, including Kinnock's personal unpopularity. Bryan Gould, however, considered that the root lay in the tax issue. In particular, he criticised the amount of time spent trying to convince electors that Labour had become 'responsible' on tax.

I was always dubious of this strategy. It seemed to contradict all that I knew about campaigning. We were playing into our opponents' hands, by using our own time to direct attention to our weakest area. I was even more aghast when, during the campaign, if ever the tax issue looked like flagging, we would go back to it by holding yet another press conference on the subject.

I was also critical of the tax proposals on the ground that they were too timid. If we were to impose tax increases, then they should at least have spared those middle income people whom we hoped to attract. There was no point in again threatening to place a cap on the aspirations of those voters, particularly in the south of England, who had found Mrs Thatcher's appeal so irresistible precisely because she offered them new horizons. A progressive tax policy should have imposed greater increases on a smaller number of people at the top end of the scale. These were, after all, the only people who had enjoyed tax gains under the Tories and there would have been little public sympathy for them if they had been required to pay some of it back.

... I was not entirely convinced that our strategy was correct, and I was not therefore totally surprised when it failed to deliver. We found ourselves bogged down on an issue which, notwithstanding Tory ineptitude, our opponents were bound to capitalise on in the end.

Bryan Gould, *Goodbye to All That*, London, 1995, pp. 247–8.

6.14   The 'wasted' Kinnock years

Not surprisingly, the 'hard' left was sharply critical of Kinnock's reforms. In this account, written by two activists, one of whom edited the monthly *Labour Briefing*, Kinnock's analysis of Labour's predicament was turned on its head. The pursuit of 'modernisation' was, they alleged, the real cause of defeat in 1992: not the fading memory of past 'extremism'.

The painful fact is that the Kinnock leadership threw away an election that was there for the taking. It did so not only in the five weeks of the campaign but in the five years preceding it. The leadership strategy of appeasing the establishment, capping working-class aspirations and taming the membership left Labour hopelessly vulnerable to the Tories on polling day. The tactic of giving no hostages to fortune in the form of clearcut policy commitments was simply an attempt to evade political realities and responsibilities – and was seen as such by the public. A Labour opposition offering fiscal rectitude, economic responsibility and little else can never hope to overturn a Tory government. In the end, Labour's safety-first approach was predicated on an assumption that the political pendulum would swing back in the Party's favour of its own accord, so long as the Party dissociated itself from past 'extremism'.

The election result was, above all, a disaster for those whose political and economic interests the Labour party exists to represent. On the morning of April 10th 1992, not a few Labour activists bitterly recalled Neil Kinnock's speech to Party conference in 1983: 'Do not ever forget how you felt on June 9th, 1983 – and say to yourself that will never, ever happen again.' But it did happen again and it will go on happening until the Party rediscovers its radicalism and its popular roots. What has to be faced is that, in this country, a general election is ultimately a test of strength between the labour movement and its party and the establishment and its party, a test whose outcome is determined by comparative strength of leadership, organization and ideology. On April 9th 1992 Labour lost, fundamentally, because on balance nine years of the Kinnock leadership had made it the weaker side in all respects.

Richard Heffernan and Mike Marqusee, *Defeat From the Jaws of Victory. Inside Kinnock's Labour Party*, London, 1992, p. 323.

New Labour? 1992–95

Labour's 1992 defeat came as a bitter disappointment. Despite a recession, the Party experienced only a slight rise in support. Kinnock's unpopularity was considered one cause of failure; Labour's taxation plans were another. Having replaced Kinnock and largely abandoned any firm spending commitments, John Smith pursued a cautious strategy and backed away from further 'modernisation' after 1993. Faced with an extremely unpopular government this seemed a prudent course to many. Smith's death in May 1994 led to the election of Tony Blair. In contrast to his predecessor, Blair considered it dangerous to expect accustomed Conservative supporters to vote Labour by default. Thus, Blair pushed ahead with further internal change and policy transformation. To this end, he revised clause iv to indicate Labour's formal acceptance of the market. Blair even referred to 'New Labour' to suggest the extent to which the Party had changed. After a year as leader, he faced increasingly vocal opposition. Few were, however, willing actively to prevent the march of Blairism. Fifteen years of opposition had caused most critics to keep their own counsel – at least until after Labour had reached Downing Street.

7.1   John Smith's cautious agenda

Neil Kinnock resigned within days of Labour's 1992 defeat. His shadow chancellor, John Smith, emerged as the unassailable frontrunner in the contest and won an easy victory over Bryan Gould. In this speech, delivered during the campaign, Smith outlined his agenda. Much of the programme continued the line developed by Kinnock. Smith's only distinctive emphasis was his support for changing the British constitution.

We live in a society which is increasingly individualistic. People define their ambitions in terms of how they can improve their own skills and opportunities, how they can provide more security for their own family, how they can improve their own home. Labour must show we are on the side of the individual against vested interests, particularly on the side of the consumer against big business. Of course individual interests are often best served by common services such as a National Health Service and public education, but we will only keep public support for them if we show we are on the side of the individuals who use them, not the institutions who provide them....

Britain is now one of the most centralised states in Europe.... I am committed to ensuring a Parliament for Scotland, an Assembly for Wales and devolution to the regions of England. I believe Britain needs a renaissance of local government to restore local democracy as a creative force for meeting local needs.... And I believe Labour must embrace the case for a Bill of Rights to protect the individual from central power....

The other task a leader must undertake is to complete the building of a membership democracy in the Labour Party on the basis of one member one vote.... Strengthening the Labour Party's democracy does not mean weakening our relationship with the trade union movement. Our values and principles are shared with the trade unions, as is our history. In modernising our systems of election and in reforming the block vote I believe we can build a new partnership with the trade union movement that will be stronger because it is fairer between Party and unions.

John Smith *et al.*, 'Labour's choice: the Fabian debates', *Fabian Pamphlet*, number 553, 1992, pp. 3–4.

7.2   The need to appeal to the 'hard workers'

> David Blunkett had been Bryan Gould's campaign manager in the 1992 leadership contest. He was a prominent MP on the 'soft' left and had given Kinnock qualified support after 1987. In an article written in the wake of Labour's 1992 defeat, he described the need to respect individualism. In so doing, he gave further evidence of Labour's adaptation to one of the commanding principles of Thatcherism.

Labour must back those who show enterprise, and whose self-reliance is not founded on indifference to the plight of others, but on self-respect and a desire for something better. People want quality public services and sensitivity to the needs of the individual and family. They don't want bureaucratic indifference or the mollycoddling of those who think the world owes them a living.

Despite enormous efforts to change perceptions, many people still see the Labour Party as offering support to those who expect the state to provide, while giving short shrift to those struggling to fend for themselves and their loved ones. Labour councils who protect tenants behaving in an anti-social fashion, while expecting longstanding and houseproud families to put up with the unacceptable, reinforce the belief that Labour has lost touch with its roots.

Historically, the Labour Party offered a voice to those who worked hard and were poorly rewarded, those who fended for themselves by building 'pathways out of poverty'. This was matched by the development of community self-help and the embryo social security system where people clubbed together to safeguard against times of unemployment or to save. The two elements of society that were not tolerated were the anti-social 'workshy' and the idle and exploitative rich.

Today's challenge is to retain a caring and compassionate approach to those in need, while responding to and representing those who wish to see their own hard work provide them with well-earned comforts. We must learn to appeal to those who are by no means rich but who, during the general election, believed Labour's appeal to them was for additional tax payments, to pass on to others. Such people, who are not against progressive taxation but don't see why they should be the ones to offer benevolence to others, not only have to be persuaded that it might be necessary for them to pay a little, but that the priorities adopted are ones they would have chosen for themselves.

Such perceptions are what is meant by a 'cap on aspirations' – where instead of reflecting and respecting the needs and priorities of the individual, Labour was viewed as looking down on or even appearing to denigrate aspirations....

Respecting self-reliance also means we should be prepared to challenge those who are in a position to make a positive contribution, but choose not to. That challenge should apply to anti-social behaviour on the housing estate as well as the board room.

New Statesman and Society, 26 June 1992.

7.3   Tony Blair's 'social-ism'

> During the campaign to succeed John Smith, Tony Blair challenged much traditional Party thinking. In this speech, he echoed the ideas of post-Crosland social democrats and also Thatcherites by suggesting that, by the 1970s, the state had become a 'problem'. In so doing, Blair prepared the ground for his later call to change clause iv.

The socialism of Marx, of centralised state control of industry and production, is dead. It misunderstood the nature and development of a modern market economy; it failed to recognise that the state and public sector can become a vested interest capable of oppression as much as the vested interests of wealth and capital....

By contrast, socialism as defined by certain key values and beliefs is not merely alive, it has a historic opportunity now to give leadership. The basis of such socialism lies in its view that individuals are socially interdependent human beings – that individuals cannot be divorced from the society to which they belong. It is, if you will, social-ism.

It is from this combination of analysis of the world as it is and prescriptions of the means of changing it that the values of democratic socialism – social justice, the equal worth of each citizen, equality of opportunity, community – came.

Once socialism is defined in this way as a set of principles and beliefs, based around the notion of strong and active society as necessary to advance the individual, rather than a set of narrow timebound class or sectional interests or particular economic prescriptions, then it can liberate itself from its history rather than being chained to it. It then no longer confuses means such as wholesale nationalisation with ends: a fairer society and more productive economy. It can move beyond the battle between public and private sector and see the two as working in partnership. It can open itself up to greater pluralism of ideas and thought....

For too long, the Left has thought it has had a choice: to be radical but unacceptable or to be cautious and electable. Whilst being 'radical' is defined as the old-style collectivism of several decades ago this may be true. But that is not really being radical at all; it is just neo-conservatism of the Left....

Once the destination – a strong, united society which gives each citizen the chance to develop their potential to the full – is properly mapped out and the ideological compass reconstructed on true lines, the journey can be undertaken with vigour and confidence. We can then go out as a Party to build a new coalition of support, based on a broad national appeal that transcends traditional electoral divisions....

The Thatcherite project of the 1980s is over. The present government has no project, except political survival. As a result the country drifts without serious purpose or coherence of direction. The prospects for a regenerated left of centre have never been better, nor its duty to grasp them greater. It is time now to rediscover our central mission of social advance and individual achievement. This is a time in which we will make our own history; not power at the expense of principle, but power through principle and for the purpose of the common good.

Tony Blair, 'Socialism', *Fabian Pamphlet*, number 565, 1994, pp. 3–7

7.4 Opposition to 'New Labour'

Ken Coates was a Member of the European Parliament and left-wing critic of various leaderships since at least Harold Wilson's time in the 1960s. In an interview conducted in December 1994, at the height of resistance to the revision of clause iv, Coates gave vent to his opinions about the Party's direction. He was apparently unaware that his comments were being recorded, hence the nature of his language. His colourful comments are a rare record of how many figures on the 'hard' left actually saw matters.

There isn't a Labour Party any more. It's finished. Tony Blair wound it up. It's gone.... I can't live without Clause 4. It's designed to remind the ancients who populate the Labour Party that they have a common root. You repudiate the common root with very, very great danger.... Why does Blair have to get rid of Clause 4? Because he has no scenario other than that if he could only get into bed with the Liberals, he could be in government for ever and ever.... He will last five minutes and then he will be disgraced because he has not one idea in his head that matters.... At the moment they [the unemployed] are going to vote Labour because they think the relief of their misery may be at hand. [But] there's no relief coming because those bastards are just going to walk past them. I can't tell you my contempt for those shits. They don't care.... The illiteracy of this generation of parliamentarians beggars the mind. They don't know anything. How can you talk about equality and assume the permanent continuation of employers and employees? What kind of freedom does an employee have? ... Bugger the next election! What difference is it going to make if we have Clarke[1] or if we have Blair?

New Times. The Journal of Democratic Left, 21 January 1995.

7.5 Labour's new aims and values

At a special conference held in April 1995 the Labour Party overwhelmingly endorsed Blair's new clause iv. This was meant to indicate to the wider electorate that Labour had changed. Critics focused on the statement that Labour worked for a 'dynamic economy', seeing this as evidence of Blair's adherence to Thatcherite thinking. However, there was much else in the new clause to satisfy even the most left-inclined Party member.

The Labour Party is a democratic socialist party. It believes that by the strength of our common endeavour, we will achieve more than we achieve alone; so as to create: for each of us the means to realise our true potential and for all of us a community in which power, wealth and opportunity are in the hands of the many not the few, where the rights we enjoy reflect the duties we owe, and where we live together, freely, in a spirit of solidarity, tolerance and respect.

To these ends we work for: a dynamic economy, serving the public interest, in which the enterprise of the market and the rigour of competition are joined with the forces of partnership and co-operation to produce the wealth the nation needs and the opportunity for all to work and prosper, with a thriving private sector and high quality public services, where those undertakings essential to the common good are either owned by the public or accountable to them; a just society, which judges its strength by the condition of the weak as much as the strong, provides security against fear, and justice at work; which nurtures family life, promotes equality of opportunity and delivers people from the tyranny of poverty, prejudice and the abuse of power; an open democracy, in which Government is held to account by the people; decisions are taken as far as practicable by the communities they affect; and where fundamental human rights are guaranteed; a healthy environment, which we protect, enhance and hold in trust for future generations.

Labour is committed to the defence and security of the British people, and to co-operating in European institutions, the United Nations, the Commonwealth and other international bodies to secure peace, freedom, democracy, economic security and environmental protection for all.

Labour will work in pursuit of these aims with its affiliated organisations such as trade unions and co-operative societies, and also with voluntary organisations, consumer groups and other representative bodies.

On the bases of these principles, Labour seeks the trust of the people to govern.

Labour Party, *New Labour New Britain: The Guide*, London, 1996, p. 60.

7.6   Blair's continuing 'cultural revolution'

Whilst some of those who supported the new clause iv hoped Blair would call a halt to further internal reform, others wanted him to accelerate change. Ben Lucas, chair of the now 'modernising' Labour Coordinating Committee, considered that, whilst abolition of the old clause had liberated the Party from a 'culture of betrayal', this was only the start.

... the Wilson and Callaghan Governments were saddled with a set of ideological expectations which they could not possibly fulfil. Tony Blair has already dealt with this problem. Changing Clause IV was not just about making Labour more electable it was about ending Labour's debilitating culture of betrayal.

Previous Labour Governments were all too often judged by activists against a set of objectives laid down in Clause IV which were utterly unattainable. Now Labour has adopted in their place a statement of aims and objectives against which the record of a Labour Government can fairly be judged.

But the culture of betrayal will only be finally banished if Labour now seizes the moment to both clarify its project and solidify support for this in the Party. This is not therefore a time for complacency. The campaign to change Clause IV has simply exposed the need for further modernisation. No one should be under any illusion that the easy victory at the April special conference reflected whole-hearted endorsement of the Blair agenda by the great bulk of party activists. The truth is not so simple.

A chasm now exists between the 100,000 new members Labour has recruited in the past year and the many activists who run the Party at local level. The new members not only embrace the change they may even have joined because of it. Whilst many of the traditional activists, by no means hard left sympathizers, were at best ambivalent. And if the contrast between old and new was clear between members and activists it was even starker between members and many trade union executives.

The campaign of persuasion which Tony Blair embarked on in the New Year must not stop with the Clause IV victory. Labour's cultural revolution is still only at its early stages. It is still a long way from becoming the participatory, empowering, listening, campaigning party which might attract people in large numbers to become actively involved in the politics of change.

Labour Activist, June 1995, pp. 1–2.

7.7 'Traditionalist' demands restated

Opponents to the revision of clause iv continued their battle against change on a number of other fronts. One such figure was Bill Morris, general secretary of the TGWU. In the period after clause iv had been changed, he faced a challenge from a Blairite candidate who stressed the need to support the Labour leadership. Despite this, Morris won re-election on the basis of policies which found little favour with the Labour leader. His victory seemed to indicate that Prime Minister Blair would face a number of problems familiar to his predecessors. Here, Morris outlines his views.

Labour is now storming ahead in the opinion polls and, while there is no room for complacency, the signs are multiplying that, whenever John Major summons up the nerve to call an election, he will lose it. So now is the time for the left to advance its own radical agenda for full employment and an end to the poverty and fear which have been the hallmarks of Tory politics over the last 16 years.

... I believe that there are four issues which should concern us most of all – full employment, ending low pay, repairing the welfare state and scrapping the anti-trade union laws passed by the Tories. These four issues stand together.

An end to mass unemployment, for example, would relieve much of the pressure on the welfare state. A national minimum wage would likewise take hundreds of thousands of families out of benefit-dependent poverty. And trade unions would be the better able to tackle poverty pay at work if they are freed from the shackles of the Tories' legislation. Unemployment, in turn, has weakened the unions as much as hostile legislation.

The whole labour movement must seize this agenda and fight for it. People must be won to positively vote for Labour on these vote-winning policies. It is time for Labour to have confidence in its own basic beliefs and core policies. Of course, the Tories will attack us whatever we say.

But every vote cast in the local council elections over the last two months said loud and clear that the British people have had enough of the Tories. They are not just rejecting the people in charge – they are rejecting the policies of the last 16 years as well.

They do not want new 'consensus' around the bankrupt ideas of Thatcherism. They want radical change.

... Any weakening of the trade unions makes the fight on almost every front harder. On the other hand, where we have managed to maintain much of our strength, despite the problems caused by the Tory laws, for example in the car industry, we have managed to win job-security agreements and pay rises in advance of the inflation rate.

... Repealing the anti-trade union laws is necessary for securing free and independent trade unionism in this country, but it is not sufficient on its own. Trade unionists need to have absolute confidence that their union will put *their* interests first and not be at the beck and call of any political party or outside organisation.

Socialist Campaign Group News, June 1995.

7.8   Blair's 'party within a party'

> Throughout the 1980s and 1990s, *Tribune* opposed most changes to Labour's programme and organisation. By the summer of 1995, above the paper's masthead appeared the slogan 'Campaigning for full employment and a national minimum wage'. This expressed doubt that Tony Blair truly favoured such policies. In this editorial, *Tribune* voiced the suspicion that Blair had, in fact, created a 'party within a party' along the lines of the SDP and was moving away from all of Labour's 'traditional' policies.

There is a crisis of confidence in the Labour Party. There is anger and discontent at the party's shift to the Right. This anger is not just to be found on the Left, it comes from the Centre and the old Labour Right. But, with a general election in the offing, few are prepared to put their head above the parapet for fear of being accused of damaging Labour's chances. This is despite the fact that the real disloyalty to Labour, its values and traditions, comes from the 'new' Right.

The Left used to be blamed for losing elections. Sections of it must bare some responsibility for the 1983 debacle. However, the Left was sidelined in 1987 and 1992 just as it is now. Then again, perhaps the whole Labour Party is out of the picture.

Last Saturday *The Guardian* revealed that Tony Blair had set up a secret committee to oversee Labour Party policy in the run-up to the general election.

Presided over by a junior whip, Peter Mandelson,[2] the group also incudes former SDP candidates Derek Scott and Roger Liddle ..., Geoff Mulgan who runs the semi-detached think-tank Demos, and Patricia Hewitt, who works for management consultants, Price Waterhouse.

Mr Blair's office denied the existence of the committee but agreed that these individuals did act as advisors and speech-writers. The denial does not alleviate the gravity of the situation. Committee or no committee, many of these same individuals have been busy helping to ensure that New Labour's stamp of social and economic conservatism appears in every Shadow Cabinet policy paper. Mr Mandelson's role as unofficial deputy leader is causing great angst within the Parliamentary Labour Party but it is the activities of those such as Mr Scott and Mr Liddle – who betrayed the Labour Party when they decamped to the SDP – and who show no contrition for what they did, which really sticks in the craw....

It is a year since Tony Blair won an overwhelming mandate to lead the Labour Party. He inherited a united party from John Smith and the goodwill of the Labour movement. Most members knew little about him but liked what they saw, even though he had little to say about his intentions. This is largely erroneous now as the fissures appear.

Mr Blair seems to want to create a new party from within. Bizarrely, this new party appears to be a *laissez faire* one, which preaches 'tough love' to the poor and the unemployed. The Labour leader even praises the 'radicalism of Mrs Thatcher'. Her radicalism atomised society, creating an inequality which rivals Victorian times.

So, can the brakes be applied? That is largely down to the Shadow Cabinet and Mr Blair's good sense. Otherwise, we are in for a rough ride.

Tribune, 21 July 1995.

7.9 Blair answers his critics

After a summer of criticism about the pace and nature of his 'modernisation' of the Party, Tony Blair used a speech to the 1995 TUC to defend his position. With Neil Kinnock sitting on the platform, Blair reminded delegates of the need to make Labour electable.

I say from the bottom of my heart, when I take the decisions I believe are necessary to put this party in the position where it can win an election, it is not because I want to turn my back on the beliefs of the party, it is because I know that if we cannot get a Labour Government we can do nothing for the poor, the unemployed and the homeless.

Of course it's hard. There is frustration building up, anger and outrage at what has happened but that is not enough. We have to have the means of translating it into a change in government.

I have sat there in the House of Commons ever since 1983 watching those people [the Conservatives] ruin our country.

Look around society and see the injustice, the opportunity denied, the unfairness, all that elitism, that establishment. Look around and see a world that has plenty yet is torn by starvation and war.

There are still great causes to unite decent people, great struggles to be won out there but what has come home to me more than anything else is the utter futility of Opposition.

I didn't join a party of protest, I joined a party of government.

Don't let anyone forget it is power for a purpose. These Tories wouldn't understand decency, respect and integrity if it came up and bit them in the leg.

I say 'new' Labour without apology or hesitation. That man there, Neil Kinnock, he struggled. He brought this party back from where it was, virtually dead.

Don't ever forget – because he won't – every inch of the way was '*You shouldn't do it. It's going too far. It's the wrong thing. It's all being run by a tiny elite.*'

But we had to do it. John Smith had to do it and I had to do it too, because the society I want to create is not some fantasy or dream.

It could be true but only if we have the guts, the discipline, the decency and honesty to tell it to those people out there like it is – not make promises we can't keep, deliver on the promises we make and rebuild this country as a great nation again.

Daily Telegraph, 13 September 1995.

Notes

Introduction

1 For more on this period see N. Tiratsoo (ed.), *The Attlee Years*, London, 1991; K. O. Morgan, *Labour in Power*, Oxford, 1984; S. Brooke (ed.), *Reform and Reconstruction*, Manchester, 1995.

2 For example: D. E. Butler and R. Rose, *The British General Election of 1959*, London, 1960; F. Zweig, *The Worker in the Affluent Society*, London, 1961; M. Abrams and R. Rose, *Must Labour Lose?*, Harmondsworth, 1960; J. H. Goldthorpe, D. Lockwood, F. Bechhofer and J. Platt, *The Affluent Worker*, three volumes, Cambridge, 1968–69.

3 S. Fielding, 'Labourism in the 1940s', *Twentieth Century British History*, 3:2, 1992.

4 S. Fielding, '"White heat" and white collars: the evolution of "Wilsonism"', in R. Coopey, S. Fielding and N. Tiratsoo (eds), *The Wilson Governments, 1964–70*, London, 1993.

5 For a critique of such a perspective, see D. Marquand, *The Progressive Dilemma*, London, 1991.

6 For the background, see R. McKibbin, *The Evolution of the Labour Party, 1910–1924*, Oxford, 1974.

7 B. Castle, *The Castle Diaries, 1964–1976*, London, 1990, p. 261.

8 L. Minkin, *The Labour Party Conference*, London, 1978.

9 L. Minkin, *The Contentious Alliance*, Edinburgh, 1991.

10 P. Seyd and P. Whiteley, *Labour's Grass Roots*, Oxford, 1992, pp. 174–200.

11 P. Whiteley, 'The decline of Labour's local party membership and electoral base, 1945–79', in D. Kavanagh (ed.), *The Politics of the Labour Party*, London, 1982, pp. 111–34.

12 Seyd and Whiteley, *Grass Roots*, pp. 32–7.

13 A. Heath, R. Jowell and J. Curtice, *How Britain Votes*, Oxford, 1985.

14 E. Hobsbawm, 'The forward march of Labour halted?', in M. Jacques

and F. Mulhern (eds), *The Forward March of Labour Halted?*, London, 1981; G. S. Jones, 'Why is the Labour Party in a mess?', in his *Languages of Class*, Cambridge, 1983.

15 D. Coates, *The Labour Party and the Struggle for Socialism*, Cambridge, 1975; J. Hinton, *Labour and Socialism. A History of the British Labour Movement*, Brighton, 1983; D. Howell, *British Social Democracy*, London, 1976, 1980 edn; J. Saville, *The Labour Movement in Britain*, London, 1988.

16 R. Miliband, *Parliamentary Socialism*, London, 1961, 1972 edn, p. 376.

17 Saville, *Labour Movement*, p. 133.

18 *Marxism Today*, April 1982, p. 41.

19 Miliband, *Parliamentary Socialism*, p. 348.

20 E. Shaw, *The Labour Party Since 1979*, London, 1994.

21 K. Jefferys, *The Labour Party Since 1945*, London, 1993; J. Cronin, *Labour and Society in Britain, 1918–1979*, London, 1984.

22 S. Fielding, *Labour: Decline and Renewal*, Manchester, 1994.

23 R. Desai, *Intellectuals and Socialism. 'Social Democrats' and the Labour Party*, London, 1994, p. 185.

24 N. Tiratsoo, 'Popular politics, affluence and the Labour Party in the 1950s', in A. Gorst, L. Johnman and W. S. Lucas (eds), *Contemporary British History, 1931–61*, London, 1990.

25 Seyd and Whiteley, *Grass Roots*, p. 188.

26 Some examples of local studies are: D. V. Donnison and D. E. G. Plowman, 'The function of local Labour parties', *Political Studies*, 2:2, 1954; F. Bealey, J. Blondel and W. P. McCann, *Constituency Politics*, London, 1965; B. Hindess, *The Decline of Working-Class Politics*, London, 1971; T. Forrester, *The Labour Party and the Working Class*, London, 1976.

27 N. Tiratsoo, *Reconstruction, Affluence and Labour Politics: Coventry, 1945–60*, London, 1990, pp. 119–20.

28 Jones, 'Labour Party', p. 239.

29 S. Fielding, P. Thompson and N. Tiratsoo, *'England Arise!' The Labour Party and Popular Politics in 1940s Britain*, Manchester, 1995.

30 G. Elliott, *Labourism and the English Genius*, London, 1993; W. Thompson, *The Long Death of British Labourism*, London, 1993; C. Hay, 'Labour's Thatcherite revisionism: playing the "Politics of Catch-up"', *Political Studies*, 42:4, 1994.

31 Shaw, *Labour Party*, pp. 103–7.

32 M. J. Smith, 'A return to revisionism? The Labour Party's Policy Review', in M. J. Smith and J. Spear (eds), *The Changing Labour Party*, London, 1992; M. J. Smith, 'Understanding the "Politics of

Catch-up": the modernization of the Labour Party', *Political Studies*, 42:4, 1994.
33 R. Samuel and G. S. Jones, 'The Labour Party and social democracy', in R. Samuel and G. S. Jones (eds), *Culture, Ideology and Politics*, London, 1982, p. 327.
34 S. E. Padgett and W. E. Paterson, *A History of Social Democracy in Postwar Europe*, London, 1991; C. Lemke and G. Marks (eds), *The Crisis of Socialism in Europe*, London, 1992; D. Miliband (ed.), *Reinventing the Left*, London, 1994; C. Boggs, *The Socialist Tradition. From Crisis to Decline*, London, 1995.
35 T. Benn, *Years of Hope. Diaries, Papers and Letters 1940–1962*, edited by Ruth Winstone, London, 1994, p. 251.

Chapter one

1 MP for Coventry East, 1945–74, and leading minister in Harold Wilson's governments of the 1960s. He was a quixotic supporter of Bevan in the 1950s but attempted to stay on good terms with Gaitskell.
2 Cripps and Bevin were respectively Chancellor and Foreign Secretary.
3 Both Baird and Evans were local MPs.
4 MP for Grimsby, 1945–59.
5 MP for Gloucestershire South, 1950–55, and Grimsby, 1959–77. A leading member of the Wilson governments of the 1960s and 1970s, he served as Foreign Secretary under Callaghan. He died in office in 1977.
6 MP for Putney, 1964–79, and Minister for the Arts, 1974–76.
7 Herbert Morrison, Attlee's deputy during the 1945–51 government, supported moderating Labour policy so it might appeal to middle-class voters.

Chapter two

1 MP for Bristol South East, 1950–83, and Chesterfield since 1988. He was a junior minister in Wilson's first government, entered the cabinet in 1966, and remained a leading member of Labour cabinets and shadow cabinets until 1983.
2 MP for Battersea North, 1946–83, and Gaitskell associate. He was a member of Wilson's cabinets until his resignation in 1967.
3 MP for Birmingham Stetchford, 1950–76, and a leading member of

Wilson's governments of the 1960s and 1970s. Jenkins was one of the original 'gang of four' Labour ex-ministers who formed the SDP in 1981, becoming its first leader.

4 This phrase, historically associated with the Fabians, indicates the confident belief that 'socialism' would evolve through the peaceful application of reforms by elected Labour administrations over a protracted period, rather than a revolutionary seizure of power.

5 MP for Smethwick, 1945–64, and Leyton, 1966–74. He held a number of posts in Wilson's 1960s governments.

6 MP for Blackburn, 1945–79, and a leading member of Wilson's cabinets of the 1960s and 1970s. She was sacked by James Callaghan when he became Prime Minister in 1976, after which she became an MEP, 1979–89.

7 Frank Cousins was general secretary of the powerful Transport and General Workers' Union (TGWU), 1956–69, MP for Nuneaton, 1965–66, and Minister of Technology, 1964–66. His active support for unilateralism at this time was crucial.

Chapter three

1 MP for Belper, 1945–70, and deputy leader of the Party, 1960–70, served as secretary of state at the DEA, 1964–66, and as Foreign Secretary, 1966–68. A perpetual thorn in Prime Minister Wilson's side, Brown threatened resignation numerous times until he finally left office in 1968.

2 MP for Lanark, 1959–83, and Clydesdale, 1983–87. Became a cabinet minister in 1968 and also served in the 1974–79 cabinets.

3 MP for Dudley, 1945–67, Postmaster General, 1964–67, and Wilson's unofficial security adviser.

4 MP for Heywood and Radcliffe, 1946–50, and Rossendale, 1950–70. Served in various cabinet posts during the 1964–70 governments.

5 Wilson was trading on the general view that the MCC (Marylebone Cricket Club) was an example of upper-class hostility to change even in the face of failure on the field. The MCC had long regarded 'gentlemen' with their own private incomes as superior to professional players who performed for a wage. This attitude was held despite the fact that the former were invariably inferior cricketers to the latter.

6 Transport House was Labour's national headquarters until the late 1970s.

7 MP for Manchester, Hulme, 1945–50, and Newton, 1950–74.

Wilson confidant and member of his 1964–70 cabinets, holding various minor posts.

8 At this time deputy general secretary of the TGWU; later, general secretary of the union, 1969–78, and an important figure in the development of Labour policy in the 1970s.

9 At the time Prime Minister of the apartheid regime in the British colony of Rhodesia; he had illegally declared independence from Britain to prevent black majority rule.

10 MP for Plymouth Devonport, 1964–92, and Foreign Secretary in Callaghan's government, 1977–79. One of the 'gang of four' who founded the SDP, succeeding Roy Jenkins as leader in 1983.

Chapter four

1 MP for Salford West, 1964–83, and Salford East since 1983; he held various ministerial posts in the 1974–79 governments.

2 The Industrial Relations Act 1970, one of the first pieces of legislation passed by the Heath government, similar in some ways to 'In Place of Strife'.

3 MP for Vauxhall, 1979–89; he had worked in the cabinet office, 1966–67, then became personal assistant to Wilson, 1967–68, specialising in economic matters.

4 Some on the Labour left thought that, such was the depth of the crisis of capitalism, the Party leadership would form a National Government in coalition with the Liberals and Conservatives. This belief was based on the historical fact that, in 1931, Labour leader Ramsay MacDonald and a few colleagues had done just that.

5 MP for Leeds South East, later East, 1952–87. Minister of Defence in Wilson's 1964–70 governments and Chancellor of the Exchequer for all Labour's time in office 1974–79. Deputy leader to Michael Foot, 1980–83.

6 At the time general secretary of the TUC.

7 MP for Liverpool, Walton, 1964–90; junior minister, 1974–75. An implacable opponent of all Labour leaderships.

Chapter five

1 Mellish, a combative Catholic on the right wing of the Party, was government chief whip, 1969–70, a post he resumed in 1974 until resigning in 1976.

2 MP for Stepney, reformed as Stepney and Poplar then Bethnal Green and Stepney, since 1964. He was a member of Wilson's

cabinet, 1967–70, and held leading posts in the 1974–79 governments. He stood for the leadership in 1980 and 1983, both times performing badly.

3   MP for Hitchin, 1964–70, and Hertford and Stevenage, 1970–79; junior minister, 1966–70, leading cabinet minister, 1974–79.

Chapter six

1   MP for Oldham West since 1970 and a junior minister during the 1974–79 governments; he held various shadow cabinet posts under Kinnock, Smith and Blair.
2   MP for Southampton Test, 1974–79, and Dagenham, 1983–94. A leading member of Kinnock's shadow cabinet, he also challenged for the leadership in 1992 but resigned later in the year to protest against John Smith's economic policy.
3   At that point policy director of the Party. He played an important role in the 'modernisation' of the Party after 1987.
4   MP for Dunfermline East since 1983, Brown became John Smith's shadow chancellor, a post he retained under his ideological twin, Tony Blair.

Chapter seven

1   Kenneth Clarke, Conservative Chancellor of the Exchequer and considered a moderate member of the Major government.
2   MP for Hartlepool since 1992 and Labour's director of communications, 1985–90. He was a prime mover in Kinnock and Blair's 'modernisation' of the Party, and the left tended to view him in diabolic terms.

Guide to further reading

Works of reference

H. Smith, *The British Labour Movement to 1970. A Bibliography*, London, 1981, provides a useful short-cut to the literature published during the period it covers. Another great help is the *Labour History Review*, produced by the Society for the Study of Labour History and published three times a year. This journal not only includes an extensive reviews section in each issue but also produces an annual bibliography of works concerned with Labour history. The *Dictionary of Labour Biography* is an on-going enterprise and contains valuable biographical material on a generous range of Labour people, both famous and obscure. C. Cook and D. Waller, *Sources in Contemporary British History*, three volumes, London, 1994, contains helpful information about collections of the papers of Labour leaders as well as those of the national Party and CLPs.

General overviews

Probably the best survey of the period for any discussion of the post-war Labour Party is K. O. Morgan, *The People's Peace*, Oxford, 1990. An adequate alternative is provided by A. Sked and C. Cook, *Post-War Britain*, Harmondsworth, 1979, 1993 edn. Of those general studies of Labour that take a broadly critical view of the Party and, in particular, its leadership, R. Miliband, *Parliamentary Socialism*, London, 1961, 1972 edn, is still the key work. Of the others, J. Hinton, *Labour and Socialism. A History of the British Labour Movement*, Brighton,

1983, but also D. Howell, *British Social Democracy*, London, 1976, 1980 edn, G. Elliott, *Labourism and the English Genius*, London, 1993, W. Thompson, *The Long Death of British Labourism*, London, 1993, and E. Shaw, *The Labour Party since 1945*, Oxford, 1996, make their own particular cases to greater or lesser effect. More sympathetic, if hardly uncritical, views are contained in K. Jefferys, *The Labour Party Since 1945*, London, 1993, and S. Fielding, *Labour: Decline and Renewal*, Manchester, 1994. Those specifically interested in surveys of Labour ideology should consult G. Foote, *The Labour Party's Political Thought*, London, 1985, H. M. Drucker, *Doctrine and Ethos in the Labour Party*, London, 1979, and N. Thompson, *Political Economy and the Labour Party*, London, 1996.

Labour in government

Labour's two post-war periods in office are the subject of an ever-expanding literature which is only slightly hamstrung by the fact that most official records cannot be viewed until after thirty years have elapsed. Concise surveys of both the 1960s and 1970s can be found in: O. Hartley, 'Labour governments, 1924–79', and K. O. Morgan, 'Symposium. The Labour Party's record in office', both in *Contemporary Record*, 3:4, 1990; D. Steel, 'Labour in office: the post-war experience', in C. Cook and I. Taylor (eds), *The Labour Party. An Introduction*, London, 1980; and M. Ceadel, 'Labour as a governing party', in T. Gourvish and A. O'Day (eds), *Britain Since 1945*, London, 1991. Most studies of the 1964–70 governments can best be divided between those which are critical and the rest, which are extremely critical. Of the latter, D. Coates, *The Labour Party and the Struggle for Socialism*, Cambridge, 1975, is especially damning, whilst C. Ponting, *In Breach of Promise*, London, 1989, is rather less so. Ponting also uses official American records to compensate for the lack of British ones. The essays in R. Coopey, S. Fielding and N. Tiratsoo (eds), *The Wilson Governments, 1964–70*, London, 1993, appreciate the problems faced by Wilson but still consider his governments to have been a failure. In contrast, B. Lapping, *The Labour Governments*, Harmondsworth, 1970, gives a positive, unashamedly loyalist view. Accounts of the 1974–79 governments follow the same pattern set by those devoted to the earlier period. Amongst the most severe critics are D. Coates, *Labour in Power?*, London, 1980, and K. Coates (ed.), *What Went Wrong?*, Nottingham, 1979. M. Holmes, *The Labour Government, 1974–79*, London, 1985, is more qualified in its judgements, as is P. Whitehead, 'The Labour governments, 1974–79', in P. Hennessey and A. Selsdon (eds), *Ruling Performance*, Oxford, 1987.

Electoral performance

The Nuffield election studies, written by D. E. Butler and various other contributors, provide the standard account of each election campaign in this period. An alternative view of the 1983 and 1992 general elections has been provided by A. Heath, R. Jowell and J. Curtice, *How Britain Votes*, Oxford, 1985, and the volume edited by the same authors, *Labour's Last Chance?*, London, 1994. Complementing these more specific accounts is the survey provided by I. Crewe, 'The Labour Party and the electorate', in D. Kavanagh (ed.), *The Politics of the Labour Party*, London, 1982. Such discussions are usefully located in an even broader framework provided by E. Hobsbawm, 'The forward march of Labour halted?' in M. Jacques and F. Mulhern (eds), *The Forward March of Labour Halted?*, London, 1981, and G. S. Jones, 'Why is the Labour Party in a mess?', in his *Languages of Class*, Cambridge, 1983.

Party divisions

Given the extent to which Party members have differed over the meaning of 'socialism' it is no wonder Labour's history has been marked by factional division. Unfortunately, for the most part, studies of these groups usually focus on personalities rather than the wider context; there is also much more on the left than the right. There are a number of accounts of the activities of the Bevanites and Gaitskellites in the 1950s. Whilst on an earlier period, J. Schneer, *Labour's Conscience. The Labour Left, 1945–51*, London, 1988, gives useful background on the left. M. Jenkins, *Bevanism. Labour's High Tide*, Nottingham, 1979, unconvincingly suggests that Bevanism was a sort of quasi-revolutionary movement; however, at least it concentrates on activities outside Westminster. M. Foot, *Aneurin Bevan, 1945–60*, London, 1973, and J. Campbell, *Aneurin Bevan and the Mirage of British Socialism*, London, 1987, battle over the significance and validity of Bevan and come up with contrasting conclusions: both should be read sceptically. Similarly, on the right, whilst S. Haseler, *The Gaitskellites*, London, 1969, praises, R. Desai, *Intellectuals and Socialism. 'Social Democrats' and the Labour Party*, London, 1994, tends to damn. B. Brivati, 'The Campaign for Democratic Socialism', *Contemporary Record*, 4:1, 1990, gives an insight into the activities of the 'hard' right in the early 1960s. Surprisingly, there is little of a specific nature on those divisions that emerged during the 1964–70 governments. One exception, N. Tiratsoo, 'Labour and its critics: the case of the May Day Manifesto Group', in Coopey *et al.* (eds), *The Wilson Governments*, makes telling points about some of the leadership's left critics. Much more has been written of the intense fractiousness during the 1970s and early 1980s. One vivid contemporary account is D. Kogan and M. Kogan, *The Battle for the Labour Party*, London, 1982. P. Seyd, *The Rise and Fall of the Labour Left*, London, 1987, and P. Whiteley, *The Labour Party in Crisis*, London, 1983, give more sober analysis. Two useful studies of the entryist left are M. Crick, *The March of Militant*, London, 1984, and J. Callaghan, *The Far Left in British Politics*, Oxford, 1987. Of divisions in the Party under Kinnock, H. Wainwright, *Labour: A Tale of Two Parties*, London, 1987, gives what now seems to be a rather naive contemporary view. The first major academic study of those social democrats who left Labour in 1981 is I. Crewe and A. King, *SDP: The Birth, Life and Death of the Social Democratic Party*, Oxford, 1995.

Organisation

The classic account of Labour's internal mechanics is R. T. McKenzie, *British Political Parties*, London, 1955. As the author was a Gaitskell sympathiser, it presents almost any form of membership activity as inherently dangerous. E. Shaw, *Discipline and Discord in the Labour Party*, Manchester, 1988, gives a good account of how the leadership attempted to maintain its control of those it considered awkward customers during this period. Two massive works, both by L. Minkin, cover two important aspects of Party organisation: first, Labour's conference in *The Labour Party Conference*, London, 1978; second, the complicated way in which unions and Party have been tied together in *The Contentious Alliance*, Edinburgh, 1991. A. J. Taylor, *The Trade Unions and the Labour Party*, London, 1987, is a useful supplement to the latter.

Members

Over the period political scientists have conducted a fair number of local studies of the Labour Party and its members. Whilst their purpose, methodologies and categories of analysis have differed widely, each gives some insight into particular parties at specific times. Amongst such works are: D. V. Donnison and D. E. G. Plowman, 'The function of local Labour parties', *Political Studies*, 2:2, 1954; F. Bealey, J. Blondel and W. P. McCann, *Constituency Politics*, London, 1965; B. Hindess, *The Decline of Working-Class Politics*, London, 1971; and T. Forrester, *The Labour Party and the Working Class*, London, 1976. P. Whiteley, 'The decline of Labour's local Party membership and electoral base, 1945–79', in Kavanagh, *Politics of the Labour Party*, attempts a broad analysis of the Party's predicament. P. Seyd and P. Whiteley, *Labour's Grass Roots*, Oxford, 1992, did everybody a great service by undertaking the one and only national survey of Party members. H. Jenkins, *Rank and File*, London, 1981, is, surprisingly, the only oral history of a CLP. Much more work needs to be done here.

New Labour?

The extent to which Labour has changed since the Policy Review is much debated. C. Hughes and P. Wintour, *Labour Rebuilt*, London, 1990, gives a breathless account of the Review that relies more on anecdote than analysis. M. J. Smith and J. Spear (eds), *The Changing Labour Party*, London, 1992, does a fairly comprehensive job of summarising the Review's impact on Party policy. The first consolidated account of the impact of the Policy Review is given in E. Shaw, *The Labour Party Since 1979*, London, 1994. The two main views of the Review are outlined in M. J. Smith, 'Understanding the "Politics of Catch-up": the modernization of the Labour Party', and C. Hay, 'Labour's Thatcherite revisionism: playing the "Politics of Catch-up"', both in *Political Studies*, 42:4, 1994. Such sober analysis should be complemented by R. Heffernan and M. Marqusee, *Defeat From the Jaws of Victory*, London, 1992, which gives an enjoyable, highly partisan, 'hard-left' account of Kinnock's reforms. As to how two leading Labour figures now think about 'socialism' in the 1990s, see the introduction to G. Brown and T. Wright (eds), *Values, Visions and Voices*, London, 1995, which suggests that New Labour forms part of a venerable ethical tradition.

Biographies of leaders

Contemporary history proceeds in the first instance through biography: such works can tell the reader much about the times in which the subject lived. There are a number of biographies, of variable quality, of Labour leaders. A series of sketches of all those up to Neil Kinnock has been provided by K. O. Morgan, *Labour People. Leaders and Lieutenants*, Oxford, 1987. K. Harris, *Clement Attlee*, London, 1982, provides a serviceable account of the subject's life. P. M. Williams, *Hugh Gaitskell*, Oxford, 1982, is deeply partisan, unsurprisingly as the author was a keen Gaitskellite. B. Pimlott, *Harold Wilson*, London, 1992, is the best of three biographies which appeared in the early 1990s. This attempted to balance past criticisms with the contemporary tendency towards sympathetic revisionism. P. Kellner and C. Hitchins, *Callaghan: The Road to No. 10*, London, 1976, is still the only study of Wilson's immediate successor; K. O. Morgan has been working on Callaghan's official biography for some time. M. Jones, *Michael Foot*, London, 1994, is a perhaps overly sympathetic account of a much-maligned leader. There is as yet no full account of Neil Kinnock's life: R. Harris, *The Making of Neil Kinnock*, London, 1984, is the best of a number of 'instant' biographies published just after he became leader. A. McSmith, *John Smith*, London, 1994, is the only biography yet to hand on the subject. J. Rentoul, *Tony Blair*, London, 1995, is the better of the two studies published mere months after Blair's election. As noted above, biographies can be a useful source, but they too often assume a top-down approach to the Labour Party. In such studies Party members, for example, appear infrequently and are usually presented in a negative light. We probably know more than enough about the Labour leadership of this period but relatively little about the Party as a whole.

Index